TESS OF THE D'URBERVILLES

From the novel by Thomas Hardy

A musical

by Alex Loveless

Additional musical arrangement and original orchestrations by Christopher Ash

Orchestrations adapted by Andy Smith

samuelfrench.co.uk

FOR AMATEUR
PRODUCTION ENQUIRIES

UNITED KINGDOM AND WORLD EXCLUDING NORTH AMERICA
plays@SamuelFrench-London.co.uk
020 7255 4302/01

UNITED STATES AND CANADA
info@SamuelFrench.com
1-866-598-8449

Each title is subject to availability from Samuel French,
depending upon country of performance.

THINKING ABOUT PERFORMING A SHOW?

There are thousands of plays and musicals available to perform from Samuel French right now, and applying for a licence is easier and more affordable than you might think

From classic plays to brand new musicals, from monologues to epic dramas, there are shows for everyone.

Plays and musicals are protected by copyright law so if you want to perform them, the first thing you'll need is a licence. This simple process helps support the playwright by ensuring they get paid for their work, and means that you'll have the documents you need to stage the show in public.

Not all our shows are available to perform all the time, so it's important to check and apply for a licence before you start rehearsals or commit to doing the show.

LEARN MORE & FIND THOUSANDS OF SHOWS

Browse our full range of plays and musicals and find out more about how to license a show

www.samuelfrench.co.uk/perform

Talk to the friendly experts in our Licensing team for advice on choosing a show, and help with licensing

plays@samuelfrench.co.uk   020 7387 9373

Acting Editions

BORN TO PERFORM

Playscripts designed from the ground up to work the way you do in rehearsal, performance and study

---

Larger, clearer text for easier reading

Wider margins for notes

Performance features such as character and props lists, sound and lighting cues, and more

---

+ CHOOSE A SIZE AND STYLE TO SUIT YOU

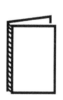

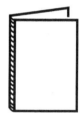

STANDARD EDITION

Our regular paperback book at our regular size

SPIRAL-BOUND EDITION

The same size as the Standard Edition, but with a sturdy, easy-to-fold, easy-to-hold spiral-bound spine

LARGE EDITION

A4 size and spiral bound, with larger text and a blank page for notes opposite every page of text. Perfect for technical and directing use

---

LEARN MORE | **samuelfrench.co.uk/actingeditions**

RENTAL MATERIALS

A Piano/Vocal Score and orchestrations are available for this production. Please see the licence agreement for the fees and conditions of hire. Please contact Samuel French for perusal of the libretti and score materials before you apply for a licence, as well as for a performance licence application.

IMPORTANT BILLING AND CREDIT REQUIREMENTS

If you have obtained performance rights to this title, please refer to your licensing agreement for important billing and credit requirements.

First produced in 2014 at the New Wimbledon Studio Theatre by Stepping Out Theatre in Association with Partisan and Fallen Angel Theatre.

ABOUT THE AUTHOR

Alex trained in musical composition at the London College
of Music and is the composer / lyricist / librettist of *Tess of the
D'Urbervilles* (New Wimbledon Studio Theatre, 2014),
Bel-Ami (Watermans Theatre / Charing Cross Theatre, 2014),
The Remains Of The Day (Union Theatre, 2010 – Evening
Standard's Critics' Choice / Time Out's Best Theatre This Month
September 2010), *Dracula* (White Bear Theatre, 2008) plus a
number of works for youth theatre. Music for plays includes
Diary of a Madman (The Century Association, New York, 2014).
Alex's work has been performed at the Park Theatre, Theatre
Royal Drury Lane, Duchess Theatre, Royal Academy of Music
and on BBC Radio 4. Alex is the recipient of a Vivian Ellis Prize
for most promising newcomer, the Howard Goodall Award for
composition, and is a professional writer associate of and reader
for Mercury Musicals Development. Alex's work is published by
Samuel French, Palgrave Macmillan and the London College of
Music where he works as a lecturer in musical theatre. His work
has been generously supported by Arts Council England and the
Big Lottery Fund.

AUTHOR'S NOTE

This musical adaptation was written for fringe production and a medium-sized cast of predominantly younger actors. The ensemble nature of the show allows for flexibility in terms of cast size and members of a larger company will discover opportunities to participate in musical numbers and as cameo roles.

Tess of the D'Urbervilles comments on issues surrounding gender; social class; and ontological schisms between science and religion, modernism and romanticism. Yet, at its heart, the book – and musical – is about one young woman's incorruptibility when confronted by material temptation. The hostile environment in which Tess's integrity is tested ultimately serves only to strengthen her resolve. Audience members may enquire of themselves the point at which they would have been tempted to compromise, had they experienced analogous conditions! Tragedy it may be, but Tess is transcendent on a metaphysical level; ultimately, like any great spirit, the world cannot hold her.

It is important that Tess is portrayed not as a victim but as the author of her own destiny. Tess brooks no compromise, wavering only temporarily in her convictions out of a concern for her family; although the path of least resistance, with its promise of social acceptability, is a continual invitation towards inertia.

Angel is guilty of dogmatically clinging to a Romantic worldview, much as he once did to a religious credo. By rebelling against his religion and exchanging one external belief system for another, he fails to emancipate himself from rigid codifications of morality. Angel's objectification of Tess contrasts with her clear-sighted view of him. She loves the man; he loves the embodiment of a myth: that of the pure peasant girl communing with nature.

Alec is a recidivist. A slave to his base instincts, he lacks any of the inner conviction or integrity necessary to harness his will. Capable of grasping only the basic tenets of morality when extrinsically motivated to do so, such shallow conviction is readily supplanted by personal desire. Tess is objectified by Alec, alternately as temptress or saviour, dependent on his mood.

Members of the ensemble are of dramatic interest only inasmuch as they interact with Tess or influence her fate. The concerns of Alec and Angel, other than those which relate directly to Tess, are of little importance as it is she who catalyses the growth of both these characters.

The overall style of the piece is expressionistic, with scenes transitioning cinematically. The mise-en-scene is created by the ensemble on a composite set, plus lighting and sound design. Properties are largely the accoutrements of Victorian country life, with the most complex acquisitions likely to be milk pails and bales of hay!

Alex Loveless

TESS OF THE D'URBERVILLES was first performed by Stepping Out Theatre in association with Partisan and Fallen Angel Theatre Company at the New Wimbledon Theatre Studio, London, on 2nd September 2014. The cast was as follows:

FELIX CLARE, JONATHAN, & ENSEMBLE . . . . Luka Bjelis

TESS DURBEYFIELD. . . . . .Jessica Daley

JOAN DURBEYFIELD, MRS CLARE

MRS D'URBERVILLE, & ENSEMBLE. . . . . .Catherine Digges

JOHN DURBEYFIELD, PARSON CLARE

DAIRYMAN CRICK, & ENSEMBLE . . . . Marc Geoffrey

RETTY, LISA LU, & ENSEMBLE. . . . . .Emma Harrold

ANGEL CLARE . . . . Nick Hayes

IZZ & ENSEMBLE . . . . Sarah Kate Howarth

PARSON TRINGHAM, LANDLORD & ENSEMBLE . . . . Guy Hughes

MARIAN, LANDLADY, & ENSEMBLE . . . . .Jessica Millward

ALEC D'URBERVILLE. . . . . Martin Neely

CUTHBERT CLARE, MAN (KINGSBERE)

POLICEMAN, & ENSEMBLE . . . . .Alex Wingfield

Directed by. . . . . Chris Loveless

Musical Director, Musical Arrangements, & Sound Design . . . . . . .Christopher Ash

Movement Director . . . . Lucy Cullingford

Stage Design. . . . . David Shields

Associate Movement Director & Period Movement Advisor . . . . Maria Clarke

Costume Design. . . . . Penn O'Gara

Lighting Design. . . . . .Phil Spencer Hunter

Stage Manager . . . . .Kiefer Bryson

Operator. . . . . .Steve Vearncombe

Voice Coach. . . . . Katie Crooks

Casting Director. . . . . .Benjamin Newsome

Production Photography. . . . . .Michael Brydon

Publicity . . . . Kevin Wilson

Graphic Design . . . . Ann Stiddard

Minimum cast of 11 (5 female, 6 male) although this can be expanded considerably. The original cast included 6 actor musicians plus two additional instrumentalists although the music can be performed by a conventional pit orchestra.

PRINCIPAL MUSICAL NUMBERS
ACT 1

PROLOGUE.............................. JOHN & PARSON TRINGHAM

CHILDREN OF THE EARTH......... ANGEL, FELIX, CUTHBERT & FEMALE
ENSEMBLE

I SAW YOUR FACE .... TESS

GENTLEMAN .... ENSEMBLE

FORBIDDEN FRUIT .... ALEC & TESS

SATURDAY NIGHT... ENSEMBLE

I HEAR YOUR VOICE .... TESS & ALEC

I COULD NEVER LOVE YOU .... TESS & ALEC

REPRISE: CHILDREN OF THE EARTH /
DOG DAYS.. ENSEMBLE

UNTIL MY HEART IS FREE...................................... TESS

DAIRY SONG... ENSEMBLE

I DEAL IN IDEALS ....ANGEL & TESS

WILL YOU MARRY ME .... IZZ, MARIAN & RETTY

PRETTY TIPPLE .... CUTHBERT, ANGEL, MRS CLARE & PARSON CLARE

A TRULY CHRISTIAN WOMAN .... PARSON CLARE, ANGEL & MRS CLARE

THE PROPOSAL...ANGEL & TESS

THE BELLY OF THE BEAST................................. ENSEMBLE

DO YOU BELIEVE IN LOVE ....ANGEL & TESS

WEDDING CHORALE .... ENSEMBLE

THE FOLLY OF MY YOUTH ....ANGEL & TESS

ACT 2

ENTR'ACTE

CARRY ME HOME .... IZZ, MARIAN & RETTY

BRAZIL........................... MRS CLARE, ANGEL & PARSON CLARE

STONY GROUND .... MARIAN & ENSEMBLE

JOYFULLY, WE PRAISE....................................... ENSEMBLE

SORROW .... TESS & ALEC

REPRISE: THE BELLY OF THE BEAST .... ENSEMBLE

REPRISE: UNTIL MY HEART IS FREE........................ TESS & JOAN

REPRISE: FORBIDDEN FRUIT .... ALEC & TESS

MAKE YOUR DECISION ....ALEC, TESS & ENSEMBLE

ONCE, I WAS YOURS....................................TESS & ANGEL

YOU LIED TO ME .... TESS & ALEC

NOW ISN'T OVER ....TESS & ANGEL

FINALE .... JOHN, PARSON TRINGHAM, TESS, ANGEL & ENSEMBLE

Running time: 2 hours 25 minutes approximately (including 1 interval of
15 minutes)

CHARACTER LIST

TESS DURBEYFIELD

Age 16–23. An unsophisticated and poor country girl with only a basic education, Tess is nevertheless a free spirit and independent thinker.

Tess has a two-octave range (G3 – G5) and needs to sing through this on a regular basis. Tess is a mezzo-soprano role and needs to be convincing and comfortable in "head" voice (above the "break"). On the one hand her range can be quite high and operatic, and on the other, she also needs to be able to sound "folky", and "authentic".

ANGEL CLARE

Age 22–29. Idealist and iconoclast who does not conform to the rigid puritanical religious tenets espoused by his parson father. Eschewing a university education like that of his brother's, Angel pursues a career in farming, meeting Tess at Talbothays Dairy where the two fall in love, and wed.

Angel is a tenor / high baritone singing up to A4 (optional) or A flat 4.

ALEC D'URBERVILLE

Age 24–31. Wealthy and worldly, domineering and debauched, Alec seduces and rapes Tess after she comes to his family home to claim kin, unaware that Alec and his ancestors are of common stock and have merely assumed a distinguished name in order to enhance their status.

Alec is low tenor / baritone singing up to F sharp 4.

ENSEMBLE

The ensemble need to cover SATB harmonies in choral work. In practice, "sopranos" can be mezzos with a good reach and "basses" can be sung by baritones.

There is potential to use the actors playing Alec & Angel during extended periods of downtime to (subtlely) enhance the ensemble.

The allocation of roles below allows the piece to be performed by eleven actors.

ACTOR 1: JOHN DURBEYFIELD, DAIRYMAN CRICK, PARSON CLARE & ENSEMBLE

Age: 40s/50s. John Durbeyfield is a middle-aged haggler who travels from place to place selling his goods, providing a meagre subsistence for his family. In ill health and often "under the influence", his and his wife's shiftlessness and negligence have not provided the most secure of upbringings for his daughter Tess. Parson Clare is a puritanical Christian, rigid in his tenets, but compassionate and empathetic nonetheless. Dairyman Crick is middle-aged, humorous, worldly though somewhat rustic and old-fashioned.

ACTOR 2: PARSON TRINGHAM, BAILIFF, LANDLORD & ENSEMBLE

Age: 20s/30s + (flexible). Parson Tringham is an antiquary, sententious and self-important. His revelation to John Durbeyfield of the latter's illustrious lineage is the catalyst for the story's tragedy. The Bailiff is a steward of Alec's family home. Lecherous in drink towards Tess, his pass at her causes a fight from which Alec extracts Tess and leads her to her downfall. The Landlord is a steadfast figure, evicting Tess's family from their long-standing home because of Tess's status as a "fallen woman". He represents society's orthodoxy and unfeelingness towards those unfortunate enough to transgress its mores.

ACTOR 3: CUTHBERT, MAN (KINGSBERE), POLICEMAN & ENSEMBLE

Age: 20s. Cuthbert is one of Angel's brothers, a Reverend at Cambridge University – Fellow and Dean of his College. A classical scholar, and following in his father's footsteps with regard to faith. The Man greets Joan, Tess and Lisa-Lu at Kingsbere following their eviction and tells them that no rooms are available to let in the town of their ancestors. The Policeman arrests Tess at Stonehenge and takes her to her prison awaiting trial and execution for the murder of Alec.

ACTOR 4: FELIX, JONATHAN & ENSEMBLE

Age: 20s. Felix is one of Angel's brothers, quieter and more self-contained than Cuthbert, but equally studious and obedient.

ACTOR 5: JOAN DURBEYFIELD, MRS D'URBERVILLE, MRS CLARE & ENSEMBLE

Age: 40s/50s. Joan is a middle-aged woman, as shiftless as her husband, with the habitual mentality of a happy child. Mrs D'Urberville is the elderly, blind head of the sham D'Urberville family. Mrs Clare is wife to Parson Clare and mother to Angel. Puritanical and somewhat lofty in thought and manner.

ACTOR 6: RETTY, LISA-LU & ENSMBLE

Age: teens/early 20s. Retty is a servant at Talbothays Dairy. Innocent, sweet-natured, and more timid than her fellow milkmaids.

ACTOR 7: MARIAN, LANDLADY & ENSEMBLE

Age: 20s/30s. Marian is a servant at Talbothays Dairy. In love with Angel, she is more of a pragmatist than her fellow milkmaids. The Landlady runs the boarding-house in which Alec and Tess reside.

ACTOR 8: IZZ & ENSEMBLE

Age: 20s. Izz is a servant at Talbothays Dairy. In love with Angel, her sparky, positive temperament enables her to better cope than her fellow maids the "loss" of Angel to Tess.

ACT 1

Scene 1
A Lane Outside Marlott *(One Evening In Late May)*

JOHN DURBEYFIELD *enters carrying an empty egg basket, worse the wear for drink. He sings to himself.*

JOHN
A MAN – HE MAY TRAVEL DOWN MANY A ROAD
AND LOOK TO THE LORD TO MAKE LIGHT OF HIS LOAD
IF HE DOESN'T LISTEN, THERE'S NOUGHT LEFT TO DO
EXCEPT SETTLE DOWN WI' A FLAGON OR TWO
O' BEER

TO DANCE WI' THE DEVIL, WHERE'ER 'E MAY LURK
IS NOT TO MY TASTE – SOUNDS TOO MUCH LIKE HARD WORK
SO I'LL SETTLE FOR A PURE DROP O' THE BREW
BE DROWNIN' ME SORROWS, BUT THEN, WOULDN'T YOU
MY DEAR?

PARSON TRINGHAM *enters, travelling in the opposite direction.*

GOOD NIGHT T'YE, PARSON

PARSON Good evening, Sir John

JOHN *takes a pace or two, halts and turns around.*

JOHN
NOW, BEGGING Y' PARDON, EXPLAIN, IF YE WILL
WE MET LAST MARKET DAY ON THE CREST O' THAT HILL
I BID YE GOODNIGHT, AND Y' MADE YOUR REPLY
'GOOD NIGHT, SIR JOHN,' AS Y' PASSED ME ON BY

PARSON
I DID

JOHN
> THEN WHAT MIGHT YER MEANING BE CALLING ME 'SIR JOHN'
> WHEN EVERYONE KNOWS I BE PLAIN
> JACK DURBEYFIELD THE HAGGLER?

PARSON It was on account of a discovery I made some time ago, whilst I was hunting up pedigrees for the new county history.

> DON'T YOU REALLY KNOW, DURBEYFIELD
> WHAT THE RECORDS SHOW?
> 'DURBEYFIELDS' WERE 'D'URBERVILLES'
> TILL NOT SO LONG AGO
> WITH WILLIAM THE CONQUEROR
> YOU LANDED ON THESE SHORES
> THAT ANCIENT KNIGHTLY FAMILY
> THAT NOBLE LINE – IS YOURS

JOHN Never heard it before.

PARSON Throw up your face. That's the D'Urberville nose and chin. Branches of your family held manors over all this part of England until you declined in Oliver Cromwell's time.

JOHN
> AND WHERE DO WE LIVE?

PARSON You don't live anywhere.

JOHN
> THEN WHERE DO WE LIE?

PARSON
> TO KINGSBERE-SUB-GREENHILL YOU CAME, BY AND BY
> IN VAULTS LINED WITH MARBLE, YOUR ANCESTORS SLEEP

JOHN
> WHILE THOSE LEFT BEHIND ARE BUT EARNING THEIR KEEP

PARSON
> TOO BAD

FEMALE VOICES (*off*)
> MM...

JOHN Hark; what's that music?

PARSON (*as he exits*) 'Tis the women's club-walking. Your daughter is one of its members, Sir John.

JOHN To be sure – I'd quite forgotten it in my thoughts of greater things.

COME AND DRINK WHILE THE NEWS IS FRESH
TO THIS NOBLE LINK, TO AN ANCIENT FLESH!
NOT A MAN IN SOU' WESSEX GOT
SUCH DISTINGUISHED BONES IN HIS FAMILY PLOT!

Scene 2
Marlott Village Green, The Same Evening

JOHN *exits.* TESS *and the younger members of the* FEMALE ENSEMBLE *enter dancing. The women wear ceremonial white dresses.*

GIRLS *(in the distance, including* TESS*)*
> CHILDREN OF THE EARTH AND CHILDREN OF THE SUN
> CHILDREN OF THE EARTH AND CHILDREN OF THE SUN
> CHILDREN OF THE EARTH AND CHILDREN OF THE SUN
> CHILDREN OF THE EARTH AND CHILDREN OF THE SUN
>
> CHILDREN OF THE EARTH
> COME SING AND DANCE – AND JOIN WITH ME
> WELCOME THE SUMMER
> BATHE IN THE LIGHT
> WORSHIP GODS OF OLD TONIGHT
>
> CHILDREN OF THE SOIL
> WHO TILL THE VALE, THE COL OR THE LEA
> LEAVE THE TOIL OF DAYTIME
> WELCOME IN THE MAYTIME
> COME AND SHARE THE EVENING – FANCY-FREE!

SOLO GIRL.   GIRLS.
> SEE THE FRUITS OF SUMMER –   OO…
>   ALL
> RIPENING ON THE BOUGH

TESS
> HEAR THE BEASTS OF BURDEN CALL

ALL GIRLS
> TIMES OF PLENTY NOW!
>
> ONE COLD THOUGHT OF A WINTER'S DAY
> IS OF NO IMPORT AS WE WEND OUR WAY
> COME ALIVE NOW THE SEASON TURNS
> AND OUR SPIRITS THRIVE AS THE MILK-PAIL CHURNS

ANGEL *and his brothers,* CUTHBERT *&* FELIX, *enter, having been walking in the country. They stop and observe the dance.*
> CHILDREN OF THE SUN
> COME FROM THE SHADOW, JOIN IN OUR SONG

SEE OUR BODIES WEAVING
SOMEHOW, STILL BELIEVING
WE CAN BE THIS WAY OUR WHOLE LIFE LONG

ANGEL

HERE'S A THING – A MAIDEN TROUPE
DANCING ON THE GREEN
I'VE A MIND TO JOIN THEIR GROUP

FELIX

SUPPOSE YOU SHOULD BE SEEN!

CUTHBERT

PAGAN RITES MADE TO ROMAN GODS
ON THESE SUMMER NIGHTS SHOULD SIT QUITE AT ODDS
WITH YOUR CREED, WOULD YOU NOT DENY?

ANGEL

IT WAS YOU WHO ENTERED THE CHURCH; NOT I!

CUTHBERT Angel!

GIRLS

CHILDREN OF THE EARTH
COME SING AND DANCE – AND JOIN WITH ME
REVEL IN NATURE
DANCE TILL THE DAWN
STAY AND SEE A WORLD REBORN!

CHILDREN OF THE SOIL
WHO TILL THE VALE, THE COL OR THE LEA
LEAVE BEHIND THE PLOUGHSHARE
LIVING FOR THE NOW, CARE
NOTHING FOR THE FATES – WE'RE YOUNG AND...

ANGEL Now this is a thousand pities. Where are your partners, my dears?

GIRL 1 They've not left off work yet. They'll be here by and by.

GIRL 2 Till then, will you be one, sir?

TESS Shh! Don't be so for'ard.

GIRL 2 Ah, 'tis only in fun, Tess.

Music. **ANGEL** *tentatively picks a* **GIRL** *to dance with. He continues dancing, exchanging partners, until he comes face to face with* **TESS**.

CUTHBERT Come along, Angel, or it will be dark before we get to Emminster.

ANGEL hesitates. He smiles and bows to **TESS** *before exiting. As* **TESS** *sings, still gazing after* **ANGEL**, *the other* **GIRLS** *return to their dancing. They are joined by* **BOYS** *from the village. The* **ENSEMBLE** *gradually partner up and exit, arm in arm, until* **TESS** *is left alone.*

TESS
I SAW YOUR FACE AND MY WORLD CHANGED WITHOUT WARNING
I SAW YOU SMILE AND THE EARTH SLIPPED AWAY
SAY, WON'T YOU STAY, SIR, AND DANCE WITH US TILL MORNING?
BEAUTY AND GRACE
I SAW YOUR FACE

WHERE ARE YOU GOING?
THE FOUR WINDS ARE BLOWING
AND WHO KNOWS WHERE OUR LIVES MAY LEAD?

I HEARD YOU LAUGH AS YOU JOINED IN THE FRAY
WHY WAS I SHY WHEN THE OTHER GIRLS WERE FAWNING?
I KEPT MY PLACE
I SAW YOUR FACE
WHERE ARE YOU GOING?
UNHEEDING, UNKNOWING
THOSE LIVES CHANGED BY A WORD, A DEED

Scene 3
Rolliver's Inn *(Later That Same Evening)*

JOHN *entertains the* PATRONS *with his antics.*

ENSEMBLE

HERE RAISE A GLASS TO A NOBLE CLAN
TO AN ANCIENT LINE - AND AN ALSO-RAN
WHO CARES IF HE'S NOT A FARTHING, CAN
YOU EVER SAY 'NO' TO A GENTLEMAN?

WOMEN

TRADES ON THOSE DISTANT DAYS
HIS TALES OF GLORY FOR A SUP

MEN

THEN, WITH HIS CHEEKS ABLAZE
HE'LL SEEK INSPIRATION INSIDE HIS CUP

ALL

HE'LL TELL THE WORLD HOW IT ALL BEGAN

SOLO MAN

THOUGH IT'S TRUE THAT I'M NOT HIS GREATEST FAN

SOLO WOMAN

BETTER TO KNOW WHERE YOUR PLACE IS –

ALL

THAN
BE DREAMING OF LIFE AS A GENTLEMAN

Fiddle solo & dance.

WOMEN

HERE RAISE A GLASS TO A GIRL WHO WOKE
THIS MORNING – FOUND SHE WERE GENTLEFOLK

MEN

SURE, IT'D MAKE MANY LADIES CHOKE
TO FIND THEY WERE REEKING OF ALE AND SMOKE

WOMEN

SHE'S MADE OF STERNER STUFF

ALL

HER KNIGHT IN SHINING ARMOUR HERE

MEN

FEEDS HER HIS ENDLESS GUFF

SOLO MAN

SHE WASHES IT DOWN WITH A   **SOLO WOMAN**
    QUART OF BEER   SHE WASHES IT DOWN WITH A
                                                          QUART OF BEER

ALL

HERE RAISE A GLASS TO A NOBLE CLAN
TO THE LORD ABOVE AND HIS MASTERPLAN
NOTHING IS MORE ENTERTAINING THAN

MEN

TO SEE HIM AT BECK

WOMEN

AS SHE KEEPS HIM IN CHECK

MEN

HE'S A BROKEN DOWN WRECK OF A –

ALL

– GENTLEMAN

Fiddle solo & dance – gradual accelerando.

JOHN A toast! To Sir John, and his wife, Lady Joan!

JOAN Give over, John Durbeyfield. I've something to tell 'ee that's come into my head – a grand project!

JOHN Hey – what's that?

JOAN I've been thinking since you brought the news, that there's a great rich lady out at Trantridge, o' the name of D'Urberville.

JOHN A junior branch of us, no doubt.

JOAN And my project is to send Tess to claim kin. She'd be sure to win the lady, and likely enough 'twould lead to some noble gentleman marrying her.

JOHN 'Twill be a very good thing. What says the maid herself to going?

JOAN I've not asked her yet.

JOHN Tess is proud.

JOAN But she's tractable at bottom. Leave her to me.

> **TESS** *has entered in search of her parents.*

TESS Mother, please come home. Father must set out t'market at dawn, and t'will take him twice as long wi'out the horse. If we don't sell the beehives now, we'll be penniless!

JOAN Tess, never could your high blood have been discovered at a more necessary moment. Do you know that there is a very rich Mrs D'Urberville living out on the edge of The Chase, who must be our relation? You must go to her and claim kin, and ask for some assistance in our trouble.

TESS Well, I don't mind going and seeing her, but you must leave it to me about asking for help.

Scene 4
The Grounds Of The D'Urberville Mansion At Trantridge

ALEC Well, my beauty, what can I do for you? Never mind me. I am Mr D'Urberville. Have you come to see me or my mother?

TESS I came to see your mother, sir.

ALEC I am afraid you cannot see her – she is an invalid. What is the business you wish to see her about?

TESS It isn't business…

ALEC Pleasure?

TESS If I tell you sir, it will seem very foolish.

ALEC Never mind; I like foolish things.

TESS I came, sir, to tell you that we be of the same family as you.

ALEC Stokes?

TESS No; D'Urbervilles…

ALEC D'Urbervilles! *(Laughs)*

TESS Our names are corrupted to Durbeyfield; but we have proof that we be D'Urbervilles. And so Mother said we ought to make ourselves beknown to you – as we've lost our horse, and are the oldest branch o' the family.

ALEC Very kind of your mother, I'm sure. Well, cousin, do you like strawberries?

TESS Yes, when they come.

ALEC They are already here.

> **ALEC** *picks a strawberry and holds it by the stem to* **TESS** *'s mouth.*
>
> TRY A BIT
> JUST A BITE
> OPEN UP WIDE AND YOU WILL TASTE DELIGHT

FEEL THE FLESH
FULL WITH JUICE
THEN, AS YOU BITE DOWN – RUNNING FAST AND LOOSE

HOW DO YOU LIKE FORBIDDEN FRUIT?
TELL ME I MUST BE A CAD TO TEASE YOU
BUT THEN, THIS VAIN IGNOBLE BRUTE
FINDS HIMSELF UTTERLY MAD TO PLEASE YOU

TESS

NO MORE, SIR
VERY NICE
NO-ONE HAS THOUGHT TO GIVE ME SOUND ADVICE
WHAT TO SAY
WHAT TO DO
WHEN I'M CONFRONTED BY A MAN LIKE YOU

ALEC	**TESS**
SAY, DO YOU TASTE FORBIDDEN FRUIT?	SAY, DO YOU TASTE FORBIDDEN FRUIT?
SOMETHING WHICH PLACES YOUR SOUL IN PERIL	
MAYBE YOUR MIND WILL FOLLOW SUIT	MAYBE MY MIND WILL FOLLOW SUIT
FAIL TO CONCEAL AND CONTROL WHAT'S FERAL!	

BOTH

SAY, DO YOU LIKE FORBIDDEN FRUIT?
SOMETHING THAT'S EARTHY – AND YET INVITING
SEE HOW A MAN OF FINE REPUTE
OFFERS A WORLD THAT CAN GET... EXCITING

Scene 5
The Durbeyfield Cottage

TESS *&* LISA-LU *are at work in the cottage.* JOAN *enters.*

JOAN So, you've brought 'em round! I've had a letter. They say –
Mrs D'Urberville says – that she wants you to look after a little
poultry-farm which is her hobby. But this is only her artful way
of getting you there without raising your hopes. She's going to
acknowledge 'ee as kin – that's the meaning o't.

TESS But I didn't see her.

JOAN You saw her son. He called you 'cousin' – he acknowledged
'ee.

TESS I will go.

JOAN That's right! For such a pretty girl, it is a fine opportunity.

TESS I hope it is an opportunity for earning money. It is no other
kind of opportunity.

Scene 6
The Journey To Trantridge, Aboard Alec's Gig

ALEC *helps* TESS *climb aboard the gig. Sound of horse's hooves.*

TESS You will go slowly, sir, I suppose?

ALEC Why, Tess, it isn't a brave bouncing girl like you who asks that? Why, I always go down at full gallop.

ALEC *thrashes the reins.*

TESS Don't try to frighten me, sir.

ALEC Don't touch my arm! We shall be thrown out if you do! Hold on round my waist!

TESS *does so.*

Let me put one little kiss on those holmberry lips, Tess; and I'll stop – on my honour, I will!

TESS But I don't want anybody to kiss me, sir!

ALEC *kisses her on the cheek and she reacts violently.*

ALEC You are mighty sensitive for a farm girl!

ALEC *reins in the horses.*

TESS You ought to be ashamed of yourself! I don't like you at all! I'll go back to mother, I will!

ALEC Well, I like you all the better. Come, let there be peace. I'll never do it again against your will. My life upon it!

Scene 7
Outside Trantridge

As **TESS** *&* **ALEC** *dismount the carriage.*

ALEC   Come now, not still sore? One thing you should know beforehand – Mother is an old lady, and blind.

Scene 8
The Drawing Room At Trantridge

MRS D'URBERVILLE *examines the inhabitants of a birdcage, which is held aloft by a* **SERVANT**, *as* **ALEC** *&* **TESS** *enter.*

ALEC Mother, may I present to you, Tess; the new farm-hand.

MRS D'URBERVILLE Ah, you are the young woman come to look after my birds? I hope you will be kind to them. My son tells me you are quite the proper person.

TESS Yes, ma'am.

MRS D'URBERVILLE Can you whistle?

TESS Whistle, ma'am?

MRS D'URBERVILLE Yes, whistle tunes.

TESS A little, maybe.

MRS D'URBERVILLE Then you will have to practise it every day. I had a girl who did it very well, but she left rather abruptly. You must begin their training tomorrow or they will go back in their piping. The servants will show you around.

Scene 9
The Estate Farm

Outside. **TESS** *feeds the fowls as she practises whistling without success.* **ALEC** *enters.*

ALEC Upon my honour! There was never before such a beautiful thing in nature or art as you look, "Cousin" Tess. I have been watching you pouting up that pretty red mouth to whistling shape, and whooping and whooping. How selfish of Mother. As if attending to these curst cocks and hens here were not enough work for any girl. How selfish of Mother.

TESS But I cannot disappoint her. She wants me particularly to do it.

ALEC Well then – I'll give you a lesson. Look here; you screw up your lips too harshly.

He whistles a few bars from the number "I Hear Your Voice".

There – 'tis so. Now try.

She does, attempting to imitate the phrase.

Wet your lips a little. Try again.

Success – she smiles. They whistle the responding phrase together in harmony.

Scene 10
A Lively Inn In Chaseborough *(Evening)*

Music and dancing. **TESS** *stands to one side as the other workers from Trantridge indulge themselves.* **ALEC** *enters to one side and watches her.*

ENSEMBLE
SATURDAY NIGHT AND WE'RE REELING
THE INN AND THE MUSIC – THE FEELING
WITH MARKET DAY HERE, WE ARE DEALING
AND SELLING OUR WARES

CHASEBOROUGH TOWN FOR A PARTY

SOLO WOMAN
THE MENFOLK ARE ALL HAIL AND HEARTY

SOLO MAN
SHE GAVE ME THE EYE FROM THE START

ALL
WE WILL WIND UP IN PAIRS!

MEN
WHO CARES IF SHE'S GOT A BABY
A HUSBAND, A BIT ON THE SIDE?

WOMEN
SHORT OF A TOOTH OR TWO, MAYBE
SO SUP IT AND SWALLOW YOUR PRIDE!

MEN
SATURDAY NIGHT AND WE'RE LAIRY
WE'RE LEERY-EYED NOW

SOLO WOMAN
LOOK AT MARY!

SOLO MAN
HE'S SCORED WITH A DOG

SOLO WOMAN
SHE'S SO HAIRY

ALL
HE MUST BE FAR GONE

SOLO WOMAN
> SATURDAY NIGHT AND HE'S BUYING

SOLO MAN
> YOU CAN'T BLAME A MAIDEN FOR TRYING

SOLO WOMAN
> YOU'LL SOON SEE THOSE PETTICOATS FLYING

ALL
> THE CLOTHES WILL STAY ON!

ALEC *(approaching* **TESS***)* My pretty, what brings you here on your day off?

TESS I came to market this morning, sir, wi' some o' the labouring folk. I have been waiting to have their company home, but I really think I will wait no longer.

ALEC Do not. Come with me and I'll take you home.

TESS I am much obliged to you, sir, but I will not trouble you.

ALEC Very well, silly! Please yourself.

MEN
> WHO CARES IF SHE'S GOT NO MORALS?
> WE HAVEN'T GOT TIME FOR SUCH QUALMS

WOMEN
> WHO CARES IF HE FIGHTS AND QUARRELS?
> I'VE STILL GOT A MAN IN MY ARMS

MEN
> SATURDAY NIGHT AND SHE'S FLITTING
> BETWEEN US – WE'RE GROWLING AND SPITTING
> WE'LL TURN IN A TRICE AND BE HITTING
> THE FIRST MAN WHO GLARES

WOMEN
> SATURDAY NIGHT AND WE'RE STUMBLING
> I CAN'T TELL A WORD THAT HE'S MUMBLING
> HIS FINGERS ARE FAST AND THEY'RE FUMBLING
> THEIR SWEET WAY DOWNSTAIRS!

SOLO

> SATURDAY NIGHT AND WE'RE REELING
> THE INN AND THE MUSIC – THE FEELING
> WITH MARKET DAY HERE, WE ARE DEALING
> AND SELLING OUR WARES

SOLO

> SING IT AGAIN…

Scene 11
The Street Outside The Inn *(Later That Night)*

The scene transforms to the street outside and the walk home. The
ENSEMBLE *sings drunkenly.*

CHASEBOROUGH TOWN FOR A PARTY
THE MENFOLK ARE ALL HAIL AND HEARTY
I KNEW HE WAS MINE FROM THE START
YE CAN TELL THAT HE CARES

                                                    SING IT A –

During the above a **MALE SERVANT**, *who is partnered with one of*
the women, leers at **TESS** *and attempts to make a pass at her. The*
WOMAN *notices this and lunges at* **TESS** *in a fury. Music. The*
scene degenerates into a fracas. A shout interrupts the proceedings.

ALEC *(enters)* I say! What the devil is all this row about, workfolk?

The fight breaks up.

MALE SERVANT Nothing, sir. Just high spirits, 'tis all.

ALEC Indeed. *(To* **TESS***)* Come with me and we'll get shot of these
    screaming cats in a jiffy! *(To* **WORKERS***)* Now, home, all of you.

ALEC *&* TESS *exit. The* **WORKERS** *break down in laughter.*

MAN Out of the frying-pan into the fire!

Scene 12
'The Chase' Woodland *(Later That Night)*

ALEC *&* TESS *walk together.*

TESS Why, where be we?

ALEC Passing by a wood.

TESS What wood? Surely we are quite out of the road.

ALEC A bit of The Chase – the oldest wood in England. It is a lovely night, and why should we not prolong our walk a little?

TESS How could you be so treacherous! I shall walk home alone.

ALEC You cannot walk home alone. We are miles away from Trantridge, if I must tell you.

Beat.

By the bye, Tess, your father has a new horse today. Somebody gave it to him.

TESS Somebody? You!

ALEC Tessy – don't you love me ever so little now?

TESS I'm grateful. But I fear –

ALEC *moves in to kiss her.* TESS *almost succumbs for a moment before struggling away.*

HOW DO I RESIST YOU WHEN YOU TANGLE UP MY THOUGHTS?
WHISPERING THE WORDS I WANT TO HEAR
PLAY ON MY EMOTIONS – SO DISTORTED, OUT OF SORTS
IT'S YOU WHO I SHOULD FEAR

I HEAR YOUR WORDS – THEY TWIST AGAIN INSIDE OF ME
AND I FEEL YOUR BREATH AS YOU DRAW NEAR
IF I SHOULD TRUST YOU – WOULD I FIND YOU'D LIED TO ME?
HOPING TO TAKE WHAT I HOLD DEAR

ALEC *(offering her a druggist's bottle – **TESS** drinks)*
   NOW I SEE YOU SHIVERING – YOUR FLESH AGAINST THE COLD
   MY DESIRE IS BUT TO KEEP YOU WARM
   TRY A SIMPLE POTION – AN ELIXIR OF OLD
   AND FEEL THE NIGHT TRANSFORM

BOTH
   I HEAR YOUR VOICE – IT TWISTS AGAIN INSIDE OF ME
   AND I FEEL YOUR BREATH AS YOU DRAW NEAR
   I THOUGHT YOU'D BE A COMFORT AND A GUIDE TO ME
   HOPED MY SALVATION WOULD APPEAR

   I CAN SEE YOU CLEARLY
   SO ENOUGH OF THIS CHARADE
   STRIP AWAY THE NICETIES OF DAY
   SHOW ME WHO YOU REALLY ARE
   BEHIND THE BOLD FACADE
   NOTHING IN THE WAY
   NO MORE GAMES TO PLAY

ALEC	**TESS**
I HEAR YOUR VOICE – IT TWISTS AGAIN INSIDE OF ME	I HEAR YOUR VOICE…
AND I FEEL YOUR HEAT AS I DRAW NEAR	I FEEL YOUR HEAT…
WHY MUST YOU FLY AND ALWAYS TRY TO HIDE FROM ME?	WHY DO I FLY?
I FEEL MY MOTIVES ARE SINCERE	WHY DO I HIDE?
I HEAR YOUR VOICE – IT TWISTS AGAIN INSIDE OF ME	I HEAR YOUR VOICE…
AND I FEEL YOUR BREATH AS I DRAW NEAR	I FEEL YOUR BREATH…
I WANT TO TASTE A WORLD WHICH WAS DENIED TO ME	I WANT TO TASTE…
SO I HAVE BROUGHT MY LOVER HERE	
SO I HAVE BROUGHT MY LOVER –	

He embraces her fully. She struggles, he restrains her, she succumbs.

Scene 13
A Country Lane *(The Next Morning)*

TESS *walks listlessly along the road towards Marlott.*

ALEC *(off)* Tess!

TESS *stops, without looking, obeying the command.* ALEC *enters.*

Why did you slip away by stealth like this? I have followed like a madman, simply to drive you the rest of the distance, if you won't come back.

Pause.

What are you crying for? Why did you come to Trantridge? You didn't come for love of me, that I'll swear.

TESS 'Tis quite true. If I had gone for love o' you I should not so loathe and hate myself as I do now! I didn't understand your meaning till it was too late.

ALEC That's what every woman says.

TESS Did it never strike your mind that what every woman says some women may feel?

I COULD NEVER LOVE YOU
AFTER WHAT YOU'VE DONE TO ME
STOLE AWAY MY CHILDHOOD
TOOK MY VIRTUE FOR FREE

WHERE'S THE MAN WHO'LL LOVE ME?
NEVER MIND MY NOBLE KIN
WHAT WILL THEY THINK OF ME
NOW I'VE SMEARED THEIR NAME WITH SIN?

I WILL NOT BESEECH YOU
FOR A PENNY MORE IN AID
I SHOULD BE YOUR SLAVE

IF I ENGAGED IN SUCH TRADE
NOW I'VE SEEN HOW THE PRICE
MUST BE PAID

ALEC

YOU – YOU CAN HOLD YOUR OWN
BEAUTY ON YOUR SIDE
YOUTH WILL FIND A WAY
TIME WILL HEAL YOUR PRIDE

TESS

I CANNOT BELIEVE YOU!   **ALEC**
DID YOU NEVER LEARN TO   YOU COULD HAVE A THOUSAND
   FEEL?   SUITORS
MUST YOU TAKE ADVANTAGE OF   MY DEAR...
   EACH HEARTFELT APPEAL?

DO YOU HAVE NO MORALS?
IS YOUR CREED SO ILL-DEFINED?   NOTHING LEFT TO FEAR...
RESTING ON YOUR LAURELS
WHILE EXPLOITING   THAT SENSE OF SHAME
   HUMANKIND
                                WILL DISAPPEAR

I CANNOT DECEIVE YOU
MAYBE OTHER GIRLS WOULD STRAY
TAKE ADVANTAGE OF THEIR PLIGHT
AND SEE THAT YOU PAY
BUT IT'S NOT IN MY NATURE
TO STAY

Scene 14
The Durbeyfield Cottage At Marlott

The music swells as **TESS** *returns home and is greeted by* **JOAN**, *who holds her in her arms.*

Scene 15
The Village Green At Marlott *(The Following May)*

Several months later, the **GIRLS** *of Marlott dance in the fields to greet the arrival of summer.* **TESS** *passes them by.*

GIRLS

CHILDREN OF THE EARTH
COME SING AND DANCE AND JOIN WITH ME
WELCOME THE SUMMER
BATHE IN THE LIGHT
WORSHIP GODS OF OLD TONIGHT

CHILDREN OF THE SOIL
WHO TILL THE VALE THE COL OR THE LEA
LEAVE THE TOIL OF DAYTIME
WELCOME IN THE MAY-TIME
COME AND SHARE THE EVENING, FANCY-FREE!

Scene 16
The Fields Around Marlott *(Harvest Time)*

TESS *at work in the fields with the other* **FARM LABOURERS**.

MEN

THE FIELDS HAVE BEEN OPENED
THE DOG-DAYS ARE HERE
THE HEIGHT OF THE SUMMER
WILL SOON DISAPPEAR
WITH HARVEST UPON US
IT'S TIME WE EARN OUR KEEP
THE GOOD SEED HAS BEEN GROWING
AND WHAT WE SOW, WE REAP

JOAN *enters with a baby.* **TESS** *stops working and takes the child.*

CAST YOUR EYES UNTO THE GROUND	**WOMEN**
NO EVIL DO WE SEE	NO EVIL DO WE SEE
SAD WHEN ALL THE FATES CONFOUND	
A MAID AS FAIR AS SHE	A MAID AS FAIR AS SHE…

ALL

WE'RE BINDING THE WHEAT SHEAF
AND SCYTHING THE CORN
WE'RE WORKING TILL SUNDOWN
AND RISING AT DAWN

THOSE FORCES OF NATURE
THAT LIE BEYOND CONTROL
DICTATE EACH WAKING HOUR
LAY CLAIM TO HEART AND SOUL

LAY CLAIM TO HEART AND SOUL

Scene 17
The Durbeyfields' Cottage

The **ENSEMBLE** *freeze as* **JOHN** *&* **JOAN** *enter in the background.*
TESS *nurses the whimpering baby.*

TESS Baby's not well again.

LISA LU *enters with a jug of water.*

LISA LU What's his name going to be?

TESS "Sorrow". I baptise thee in the name of the Father, and of the
Son, and of the Holy Ghost. *(To* **LISA LU***)* Say "Amen".

LISA LU Amen.

ENSEMBLE
OO...

TESS *(during above)* We receive this child and do mark him with the
sign of the cross. May he fight against sin, the world and the
devil, and be a faithful soldier and servant unto his life's end.
Amen.

As the lights fade the baby's crying reaches a crescendo, and then
suddenly stops.

Scene 18
The Village Chapel

Lights up on TESS *with* PARSON TRINGHAM.

TESS Will it be just the same as if you had baptised him?

PARSON My dear girl, it will be just the same.

TESS Then will you give him a Christian burial?

PARSON The child was born out of wedlock...

TESS O, for pity's sake!

> TESS *kneels before him.* PARSON TRINGHAM *does not respond.*

Then I'll never come to your church no more!

> TESS *runs, then stops.*

Perhaps it will be just the same for him if I do it? Don't for God's sake speak as saint to sinner, but as you yourself to me myself!

PARSON It will be just the same.

Scene 19
The Graveside, Off The Churchyard Proper,
On Unconsecrated Ground

TESS *kneels as she tends the grave.*

TESS

UNTIL MY HEART IS FREE
AND UNTIL MY DYING DAY
MY LIFE IS NOT MY OWN
THE PAST IS HERE TO STAY

HOW CAN I LEAVE YOU
HERE IN UNHALLOWED EARTH?
THEY WON'T RECEIVE YOU
FAR LESS REPRIEVE YOU – MARKED FROM BIRTH

UNTIL MY HEART IS FREE
I MUST JOURNEY ON ALONE
WHERE NO-ONE KNOWS MY FACE
MY STORY IS UNKNOWN

FAR FROM THE EYES AND BABBLING BROOKS
FAR FROM THE LIES AND PITIED LOOKS
FARM-BOYS AND CLATTER
WIVES WITH THEIR CHATTER
THAT'S HOW THE SPIRIT DIES!

Scene 20
The Journey To Talbothay's Dairy

JOAN *enters with a coat and basket for* **TESS**. *They embrace.* **TESS**
sets out alone.

HOW CAN YOU HOLD ME
TO YOUR ETERNAL PLAN?
WHEN NO-ONE TOLD ME
TILL THEY WOULD SCOLD ME – WHAT IS MAN!

UNTIL MY HEART IS FREE
OF YOUR COLD INHUMAN CREED
MY GOD WILL WALK ON EARTH
WILL FEEL AND THINK AND BLEED

ALL UNTIL MY HEART IS FREE!

Scene 21
Talbothay's Dairy – The Cow Shed

The farm-hands, including **ANGEL CLARE**, *sit on stools, milking with* **DAIRYMAN CRICK** *supervising the proceedings.*

WOMEN

> HEIFERS RANGED ALONG THE COWSHED
> WITH UDDERS SWOLLEN AND REPLETE
> SQUEEZING AND TEASING
> THE MILK FROM EACH TEAT

SOLO

> SOME OF US HAVE GOT OUR FAVOURITES

SOLO

> WHILE OTHERS TAKE 'EM AS THEY COME

SOLO

> GRASPING AND CLASPING

WOMEN

> OUR FINGERS TURN NUMB
> SO PASS THE HOURS WITH A SONG OR TWO OF DAYS GONE BY

MEN

> THEN, FROM THE BOWERS, COMES THE TWITTER OF BIRDS AS A
>   FOND REPLY

WOMEN

> SOME GIVE UP THEIR BOUNTY EASY

MEN

> STILL OTHERS WORK YOU TO THE BONE

SOLO

> SQUIRTING –

SOLO

> OR SPURTING

ALL

WITH TEATS HARD AS STONE

ANGEL

CAREFUL WHEN YOU MOVE THEM ONWARDS

SOLO

HOW IS THIS DELICATELY PUT?

SOLO

PATTING AND SPLATTING

ALL

SO WATCH UNDERFOOT!

SO THEY YIELD, WE TEND THE FIELD
REMOVE EACH GARLIC BLADE
'LESS THE CREAM SHOULD MAKE YOU SCREAM
AND WONDER HOW 'TWAS MADE!

SOLO

SO WE GET THE FINEST PRODUCE

SOLO

THEY GRAZE UPON A LOWLAND MEAD

SOLO

PAMPERED

SOLO

UNHAMPERED

ALL

THEY FORAGE AND FEED

SOLO

THEN WE TAKE THEM TO THE COWSHED

SOLO

ENCOURAGE THEM TO MAKE THEIR WAY

SOLO

THRASHING –

SOLO

AND SPLASHING

ALL

UNTIL THEY OBEY

Dance break.

TEATS IN HAND, OUR LIVES ARE GRAND
AND WHO COULD ASK FOR MORE?
MILK AND CHEESE WHENE'ER WE PLEASE
WITH CURDS AND WHEY GALORE

NOT A DAY GOES BY WITHOUT US
REPLENISHING THE STOCK IN TRADE
KEEPING THEM SEEPING
AND MAKING THE GRADE

WHAT WE TAKE WE SHIP TO LONDON
AND LET THE GENTLEFOLK DECIDE

WOMEN

FATTER –

ALL

OR THINNER
WITH BREAKFAST OR DINNER
THE SAINT OR THE SINNER
WE SERVE THEM UNSWERVINGLY WITH PRIDE
WITH PRIDE
WITH PRIDE!

TESS *enters and approaches* **DAIRYMAN CRICK***, who* ***whistles*** *a few bars of the above.*

CRICK You must be Tess. Dairyman Crick – I got y'mother's letter. I knowed your mother very well when she were a young 'un. A little bird told me that the family yer mother married into came originally from these parts, and that 'twere a old ancient race that had all but perished off the earth.

TESS Oh, no, sir…

CRICK 'Tis just as well for you, mind, if it in't true. Mr Clare, my young gentleman apprentice 'ere, is one of the rebellest rozums you ever knowed; and if there's one thing that he do hate more than another 'tis the notion of what's called a' old family.

ANGEL *(attempting to milk a cow)* I merely postulate, Mr Crick, that it stands to reason old families have done their spate of work in past days, and can't have much left in them now.

CRICK Ah! Didn't I tell ye! What a rozum! Take it gentle, sir, take it gentle. 'Tis knack, not strength, that does it.

ANGEL So I find. I think I have finished her, however, though she made my fingers ache.

CRICK We've hard ones and we've easy ones, like other folks. You can try your hand upon she, maidy. You can milk her clean.

TESS Yes, sir.

> TESS *takes* ANGEL*'s place and he watches her work. One of the maids [*IZZ*] sneezes and wipes her hands on her pinafore.*

CRICK For heaven's sake, pop thy hands under the pump, Izz. Upon my soul, if the London folk only knowed of thee and thy slovenly ways, they'd swaller their milk and butter more mincing than they do a'ready; and that's saying a good deal.

Scene 22
The Same *(Later)*

ANGEL *sits reading as* TESS *enters with a milk pail.*

ANGEL I have seen you somewhere before. Where was it, pray?

TESS A village called Marlott, sir. You came walking there one day, with two other young gentlemen.

ANGEL Of course! The dance on the village green. Come, sit with me.

TESS Oh, no sir!

ANGEL Are you afraid?

TESS Well – yes, sir.

ANGEL What of?

TESS I couldn't quite say.

ANGEL The milk turning sour?

TESS No…

ANGEL Life in general?

TESS Yes, sir.

ANGEL Ah – so am I, very often. This hobble of being alive is rather serious, isn't it?

HOW DO YOU SURVIVE WHEN A NAMELESS FEAR
TAKES A HOLD AND SHAPES YOUR EXISTENCE?
FEAR OF THE DARK
FEAR OF OURSELVES
ARE YOU AFRAID OF ME?

I DEAL IN IDEALS
I CLING TO MY DREAMS
THOUGH NOTHING I'VE STUDIED IS QUITE WHAT IT SEEMS
I DELVE INTO WORDS
I TEASE OUT EACH FACT
IN HOPE THIS WILL COLOUR THE WAY THAT I ACT

HOW CAN I
LIVE OR DIE

WITH SUCH PROFOUND UNCERTAINTY?
SHINE A LIGHT
TELL BLACK FROM WHITE
THE TRUTH WILL SET US FREE

I DEAL IN IDEALS
I LEARN FROM THE PAST
THROUGH SCIENCE I HOPE THAT I'LL TRIUMPH AT LAST
I LIVE FOR THE EARTH
I REACH FOR THE SKY
I DON'T NEED RELIGION TO ANSWER THE "WHY"

I KNOW HOW IT FEELS
THOSE WHEELS WITHIN WHEELS
I DEAL IN IDEALS

Interlude as **TESS** *draws close to* **ANGEL** *– there is the sense of days passing by as* **ANGEL** *reads to her from his books.*

BOTH

HOW CAN I
LIVE OR DIE
WITH SUCH PROFOUND UNCERTAINTY?
SHINE A LIGHT
TELL BLACK FROM WHITE
THE TRUTH WILL SET US FREE

I DEAL IN IDEALS
I LEARN FROM THE PAST
THROUGH KNOWLEDGE I HOPE THAT I'LL TRIUMPH AT LAST
I LIVE FOR THE EARTH
I REACH FOR THE SKY
I DON'T NEED RELIGION TO ANSWER THE "WHY"

ANGEL

I KNOW HOW IT FEELS

TESS

THOSE WHEELS WITHIN WHEELS

BOTH

I DEAL IN IDEALS

Scene 23
The Farmyard / The Maids' Living Quarters

In the farmyard, **ANGEL** *strips to the waist and washes. The* **MAIDS** *look on from inside their living quarters.*

RETTY Don't push! You can see as well as I!

IZZ 'Tis no use for you to be in love with him, Retty Priddle. His thoughts be of other cheeks than thine!

MARIAN You needn't say anything, Izz. For I saw you kissing his shade.

RETTY She did *what?*

MARIAN Why – he was standing over the whey tub, and the shade of his face came upon the wall behind, close to Izz, who was standing there. She put her lips against the wall and kissed the shade of his mouth!

RETTY O Izz Huett!

IZZ Well, there was no harm in it. I would marry him tomorrow!

MARIAN So would I!

RETTY And I!

IZZ

> WILL YOU MARRY ME – I'M A FAITHFUL FARM-GIRL
> I CAN TILL A FIELD – I WOULD WORK FOR FREE
> YOU – A GENTLE SORT
> ME – I WOULDN'T WORRY
> KNEE-DEEP IN SLURRY
> WILL YOU MARRY ME?

MARIAN

> WILL YOU MARRY ME – WE CAN BREED TOGETHER
> LAMBS AND CALVES AND COLTS – WHAT A PAIR WE'D BE
> NOW IT'S NICE AND TAUT
> LET ME FEEL THAT MUSCLE!

RETTY *sounds her revulsion.*

> SORRY TO HUSTLE!
> WILL YOU MARRY ME?

RETTY

WILL YOU MARRY ME – THOUGH I'M NO FINE LADY
YOU – A PARSON'S SON – THERE'S NO HOPE, YOU SEE…

RETTY *dissolves in tears.*

MARIAN

POOR THING'S OVERWROUGHT

IZZ

ONLY THING I KNOW IS

MARIAN & IZZ

OUR YOUNG ADONIS
WILL NOT MARRY ME

IZZ

JUST A PASSING THOUGHT –
WE COULD GET HIM PIE-EYED!

MARIAN & IZZ

COME NOW, BE DRY-EYED

ALL

HE'LL NOT MARRY THEE!

Scene 24
The Dairy *(Later The Same Day)*

The **MAIDS** *&* **TESS** *at work.*

MARIAN *(to* **TESS***)* He likes 'ee best – the very best! He would kiss 'ee, if you encouraged him to do it, ever so little.

TESS Do you dislike me for it?

RETTY I don't know. I want to hate 'ee, but I cannot.

IZZ That's how I feel.

TESS He ought to fancy one of you. You are all better women than I.

> **TESS** *sobs.*

RETTY We better than you?

MARIAN *(to* **IZZ***)* Get some water. She's upset by us, poor thing.

> **IZZ** *runs out but stops as* **DAIRYMAN CRICK** *enters.*

CRICK Now then, maidy. What's all this?

MARIAN 'Tis the heat, sir.

RETTY Come now, Tess, you wouldn't want Mr Clare to see you like this.

CRICK You needn't worry y' heads about him. Mr Clare has gone home to Emminster to spend a few days wi' his kinsfolk. He's getting on towards the end of this time wi' me and so I suppose he is beginning to see about his plans elsewhere.

IZZ How much longer is he to bide here?

CRICK He'll bide to get a little practice in the calving out at the straw-yard, for certain. He'll hang on till the end of the year I should say.

DAIRYMAN CRICK *exits.*

MARIAN I wonder what she is like – the lady they say his family have looked out for him.

TESS Some lady looks out for him?

MARIAN Oh yes – 'tis whispered; a young lady of his own rank; a Doctor of Divinity's daughter near his father's parish of Emminster; he don't much care for her, they say. But he is sure to marry her.

Scene 25
Outside The Parsonage At Emminster

ALEC *&* PARSON CLARE *step out from the parsonage. The two men shake hands.* ALEC *turns and leaves.* ANGEL *enters.*

ANGEL Father!

PARSON CLARE *&* ANGEL *embrace.*

Who was that gentleman?

PARSON CLARE A young squire by the name of D'Urberville. Recently his mother passed away and he came to me seeking solace.

ANGEL Not one of the ancient D'Urbervilles of Kingsbere?

PARSON CLARE Oh no. This seems to be a new family which has taken the name. For the credit of the former knightly line, I hope they are spurious, I'm sure.

ANGEL How so?

PARSON CLARE That young man is possessed by the most reckless passions. I have been doing what I can to guide him and only hope that a few poor words of mine may spring up in his heart as good seed some day.

MRS CLARE *enters.*

MRS CLARE Angel, my dear boy!

ANGEL *embraces her and opens his bag to reveal black puddings and a bottle of mead, which he passes to* MRS CLARE.

Scene 26
Inside The Parsonage *(Dining Room)*

The **CLARE** *household.* **CUTHBERT** *and* **FELIX** *also present.*

CUTHBERT

SO I SUPPOSE IT'S FARMING THEN
FOR WHAT WE SOW, WE REAP
SOME OF US GO TO SHEPHERD MEN
WHILST OTHERS STICK TO SHEEP

ANGEL

AS A CONTENTED DOGMATIST
YOU MIGHT BE MORE CONCERNED
BY EVERY METAPHOR YOU'VE MISSED
THE STONES THAT GO UNTURNED

ANGEL *scans the table.*

WHERE'S THE BLACK PUDDING?

MRS CLARE

WE OFFERED IT, MY CHILD
TO A POOR FAMILY, THE MAN OF WHOM WAS WILD

HOW WE DID PRAY TO GOD ABOVE
TO CURE HIM OF HIS THIRST
ONE OF THOSE WRETCHED CASES OF –

PARSON & MRS CLARE

DELIRIUM TREMENS

MRS CLARE

NOW YOU ARE LOOKING FOR THE MEAD

PARSON CLARE

WE FOUND IT RATHER STRONG

MRS CLARE

SO IT IS STORED IN CASE THE NEED
FOR MEDICINE COMES ALONG

ANGEL

SHAME, THAT IS ONE PRETTY TIPPLE OF A BREW

CUTHBERT & **FELIX** *look up.*

CUTHBERT

WHAT DID YOU SAY?

ANGEL

I'VE PICKED UP A PHRASE OR TWO…

CUTHBERT Hmm…

Scene 27
The Same *(Later)*

ANGEL, PARSON *&* MRS CLARE *are present.*

PARSON CLARE As far as worldly wealth goes, you will no doubt stand far superior to your brothers in a few years.

ANGEL When I start in business I shall need someone to take care of the domestic side of the establishment. Would it not be as well, therefore, for me to marry?

PARSON CLARE Indeed, the idea does not seem unreasonable.

ANGEL What kind of wife do you think would be best for me as a thrifty hard-working farmer?

PARSON CLARE

A TRULY CHRISTIAN WOMAN
WHOSE MORAL SENSE IS SOUND
A TRULY CHRISTIAN WOMAN
AND SUCH AS THIS IS FOUND
EMBODIED IN THE FIRSTBORN
OF MY FRIEND DR CHANT
HIS PIOUS DAUGHTER MERCY
IS FREE FROM WICKED CANT

ANGEL But, Father, don't you think that a young woman equally pure and virtuous as Miss Chant, but one who understands the duties of farm life would suit me infinitely better?

PARSON CLARE And you have found such a woman?

ANGEL

A TRULY CHRISTIAN WOMAN
WHO KNOWS OF RURAL LIFE
SHE LIVES WHAT PAPER POETS WRITE
THE PERFECT FARMER'S WIFE
BOTH SIMPLE – AND ACCOMPLISHED
IN TASKS THAT MAY PERTAIN
TO MY NEWFOUND VOCATION
A PERFECT MATCH – IT'S PLAIN

MRS CLARE Is she of a family such as you would care to marry into – a lady, in short?

ANGEL She is not what in common parlance is called a lady, for she is a cottager's daughter. But she is an unimpeachable Christian; of the very tribe, genus and species you desire to propagate.

MRS CLARE O Angel, you are mocking!

PARSON CLARE Do not be too hasty, Angel. Your mother only desires that which is best for you.

PARSON CLARE & ANGEL	MRS CLARE
A TRULY CHRISTIAN WOMAN	BUT WHAT OF SOCIAL CLASS?
WHO'LL HONOUR AND OBEY	WHAT OF BREEDING?
A TRULY CHRISTIAN WOMAN	WHAT WILL ALL THE NEIGHBOURS HAVE TO SAY?
WHO'LL LOOK TO YOU / ME EACH DAY	THINK, MY DEAR, BEFORE YOU ACT
SHE'LL FOLLOW IN YOUR / MY FOOTSTEPS	SHE MAY BE THE BEST YOU'VE FOUND SO FAR
A PATH BOTH STRAIGHT AND SURE	THERE'S A WORLD OUT THERE
A TRULY CHRISTIAN WOMAN	AND, IF YOU RESIST THE SIREN'S SONG
WHO'S VIRTUOUS AND PURE	ITS BASE ALLURE

ALL

A TRULY CHRISTIAN WOMAN
WHO'S VIRTUOUS AND PURE

Scene 28
The Journey Back To Talbothay's

ANGEL *races back to the dairy.*

Scene 29
The Farmyard

TESS *is skimming the milk.* **ANGEL** *creeps up on her and clasps her in his arms.* **TESS** *struggles.*

TESS O Mr Clare! How you frightened me – I –

ANGEL Forgive me, Tess! I ought to have asked. I – did not know what I was doing. I wish to ask you something of a practical nature.

> WILL YOU MARRY ME – AS A FARMER'S WIFE – NO...
> WILL YOU MARRY ME – IT COULD WORK, YOU SEE...
> YOU CAN MANAGE FARMS
> WELL – WITH ME ABOVE YOU
> OH, TESS, I LOVE YOU!
> WILL YOU MARRY ME?

TESS *(out)*
> I CANNOT BELIEVE THIS!
> HAVE I NOT BEEN TRIED
>   BEFORE?
> AM I STILL FOUND WANTING
> THAT YOU ASK ME FOR MORE!   **ANGEL**
>   TESS...

(to **ANGEL***)*

> OH, MY LORD, I LOVE YOU
> BUT I CANNOT BE YOUR WIFE

                                        Are you engaged?

> I'M NOT WORTHY OF YOU
> I HAVE LIVED A LOWLY LIFE

                                        That's not the point!

> BUT YOUR FAMILY HONOUR
> IS AT STAKE –

ANGEL
>I DO NOT CARE!
>LET THEM SAY I'M HELL-BOUND
>FOR MY BROTHERS ARE FAIRLY
>CONVINCED THAT I'M ALREADY THERE!

Will you not accept me as a husband?

TESS I cannot!

ANGEL But you will make me happy!

TESS Ah – you think so, but you don't know.

ANGEL Then tell me!

TESS I will give you my reasons tomorrow – when we take the milk to the station.

Scene 30
A Country Railway Station *(Evening)*

A headlamp and steam. The **ENSEMBLE** *load milk pails on to a train.* **TESS** *and* **ANGEL** *stand to one side, observing.*

ENSEMBLE
INTO THE BELLY OF THE BEAST
INTO THE HEAT OF SMOKE AND FIRE
EACH DAY OUR OFFERING IS INCREASED
SATING THE CYCLOPS'S BASE DESIRE

INTO THE HEART OF LONDON TOWN
WHEN WILL THE GODS OF STEEL DECIDE
TO COME AND TEAR OUR FOREST DOWN?
NOWHERE FOR SIMPLE SOULS TO HIDE

INTO A WORLD OF SWEAT AND BLOOD

MEN
MAN AND MACHINE ARE JOINED AS ONE

WOMEN
THEN, WHEN IT'S TAKEN ALL THAT'S GOOD

ALL
IT'S GONE...

Sound of a train whistling and departing.

TESS Londoners will drink it at their breakfasts tomorrow, won't they? Strange people we have never seen. Who don't know anything of us, and where it comes from, or think how we two drove miles across the moor tonight that it might reach 'em in time?

ANGEL We did not drive entirely on account of those precious Londoners. Now, Tess, your heart belongs to me already, does it not?

TESS O yes – yes!

ANGEL Then, if your heart does, why not your hand?

TESS But my history. I want you to know it — you will not like me so well! There is something very peculiar about me. I – I – am not a Durbeyfield, but a D'Urberville.

ANGEL Well – why should I love you less after knowing this?

TESS I was told that you hated old families.

ANGEL I hate the aristocratic principle. However, I rejoice in your descent. Society is hopelessly snobbish. My mother, too, poor soul, will think so much better of you on account of it. Tess, you must spell your name correctly – D'Urberville – from this very day. Why dozens of mushroom millionaires would jump at such a possession. By the bye, my father told me of one young upstart who has taken the name – a certain Alec D'Urberville.

TESS Angel, I think I would rather not take the name! It is unlucky, perhaps!

ANGEL Then, Mistress Teresa D'Urberville –

SAY THE WORD AND TELL ME
THAT YOU'LL BE MINE ALONE
WHY SHOULD YOU FACE LIFE UPON YOUR OWN?

LET YOUR HEART SURRENDER
REMOVE THAT CAREWORN FROWN
TAKE MY NAME AND CAST YOUR BURDEN DOWN

DO YOU BELIEVE IN LOVE?
DO YOU BELIEVE IN PERFECT HARMONY?
AN INWARD RECOGNITION FROM THE START
WHY MUST WE ACT LIKE STAR-CROSSED LOVERS?
OUR LIVES FIT HAND IN GLOVE
SAY, DO YOU BELIEVE IN LOVE?

ANGEL & TESS
AND ALL THE WORLD IS WAITING
TO FIND THEMSELVES MADE WHOLE

ANGEL
THAT MYSTICAL TRANSCENDENCE OF THE SOUL

TESS
BEYOND OUR CONTROL...

BOTH
DO YOU BELIEVE IN PERFECT HARMONY?
A FORCE THAT BINDS US CLOSE WHEN WE'RE APART

ANGEL

DO YOU BELIEVE IN ANCIENT WISDOM?
IN FATE OR GOD ABOVE?
SAY, DO YOU BELIEVE IN LOVE?

They embrace.

ANGEL
SHALL WE EMBARK ON LIFE TOGETHER?

TESS
THAT'S ALL I'M DREAMING OF

BOTH
SAY, DO YOU BELIEVE IN LOVE?

ANGEL
SAY, DO YOU BELIEVE IN LOVE?

Scene 31
The Cottage At Marlott

JOAN *enters, reciting a letter she has written to* TESS.

JOAN Dear Tess, we are all glad to hear that you are to be married soon. But with respect to your question, Tess, I say very strong, that on no account do you say a word of your bygone trouble to him. Many a woman – some of the highest in the land – have had a trouble in their time; and why should you trumpet yours when others don't trumpet theirs? No girl would be such a fool, especially as it is not your fault at all. So no more at present, and with kind love to your young man. – From your affectionate mother, Joan Durbeyfield.

Scene 32
The Maids' Quarters At Talbothay's *(Wedding Day)*

The **MAIDS** *help* **TESS** *prepare for the wedding.*

MARIAN Are you ready?

TESS Yes.

IZZ Going to marry him – a gentleman! How it do seem!

RETTY You will think of us when you be his wife, Tess, and of how we told 'ee that we loved him, and how we tried not to hate you, and could not hate you, because you were his choice, and we never hoped to be chose by him.

TESS He ought to have had one of you! I think I ought to make him even now.

Scene 33
Angel's Quarters At The Same

TESS *bursts in as* ANGEL *dresses.*

TESS I am so anxious to talk to you – I want to confess all my faults and blunders!

ANGEL Well, you shall tell me anything – as soon as we are settled in our lodging. I, too, will tell you my faults then. But do not let us spoil the day with them.

TESS Then you don't wish me to, dearest?

ANGEL I do not, Tessy, really.

He kisses her, lightly. Wedding bells sound.

Scene 34
Outside A Church *(Later That Day)*

TESS *and* **ANGEL** *exit the church.*

ENSEMBLE *(as the congregation)*
WEDDING BELLS ARE RINGING

WOMEN
LIFT UP YOUR HEARTS IN A SONG OF GLAD TIDINGS AND PRAISE

ALL
HEAR THE VOICES SINGING

WOMEN
NOW SHE HAS VOWED TO BELONG TO HIM ALL OF HER DAYS

ALL
HOW THEY DEPEND ON EACH OTHER
CONSTANT IN SICKNESS AND HEALTH
LEARNING TO TEND TO ANOTHER
STEADFAST THROUGH HARDSHIP OR WEALTH

WEDDING BELLS ARE PEELING

WOMEN
HEAVENLY BLESSINGS ABOUND – MAY YOU PROSPER AND THRIVE

ALL
IN YOUR FELLOW-FEELING

WOMEN
ALL OF OUR FEARS GO TO GROUND AS THE HEART COMES ALIVE

Scene 35
An Old D'Urberville Mansion

ANGEL Welcome to one of your ancestral mansions! Most of it's been demolished; it's nought but a farmhouse now. But it's ours – for the next fortnight, at least!

He produces a gift box.

Mrs Angel Clare!

OFFSTAGE VOICES
OO...

Music. **TESS** *opens the package to reveal a bejewelled necklace. She looks at* **ANGEL** *who gestures for her to put it on. She does so and stands so that he can see her. He approaches her and gently adjusts her bodice to expose her throat. They go to kiss but there is a knock at the door.*

JONATHAN *(off)* Mr Clare!

ANGEL Ah. That'll be Jonathan with the luggage.

JONATHAN *(as he enters with their cases)* Forgive my lateness, sir, but we've all been gallied at the dairy at what might ha' been a most terrible affliction since you and your Mis'ess left us this afternoon. Poor little Retty Priddle hev tried to drown herself.

ANGEL No! Why, she bade us goodbye with the rest...

JONATHAN The waterman, on his way home, noticed something by the Great Pool; 'twas her bonnet and shawl packed up. In the water he found her. He and another man brought her home, thinking a' was dead; but she came round by degrees. And Marian has been found dead drunk by the withy-bed – the Dairyman hev threatened to dismiss 'er.

TESS And Izz?

JONATHAN Izz is about house as usual; but she seems to be very low in mind about it, poor maid, as well she mid be. Sorry to be the bearer o' such bad tidings, Misuss, on today o' all days.

JONATHAN *exits.*

ANGEL I am so sorry you should have heard this sad story about the girls. Poor Retty. Some people are naturally morbid without the least cause.

TESS While they who do have cause to be, hide it, and pretend they are not.

ANGEL Do you remember what we said to each other this morning about telling our faults? I want to make a confession to you, Love. I did not tell you before because I was afraid of endangering my chance of you, darling, the great prize of my life. I wonder if you will forgive me?

I HAD A FAITH – FROM CHILDHOOD TEACHING
YET I REBELLED AND TURNED AWAY
I'D HAD MY FILL OF PIOUS PREACHING
THOUGHT I KNEW BETTER IN THE DAY

LOST AND ALONE, MY HEART WAS YEARNING
FOR SOMETHING REAL THAT I COULD TRUST
I WAS TOO YOUNG TO BE DISCERNING
I WAS CONSUMED BY PRIDE AND LUST

TRAVELLED TO LONDON – FOUND A WOMAN
ACTIONS IMPROPER AND UNCOUTH
LED TO MY UNTIMELY FALL
BUT I SWEAR THAT THIS WAS ALL
BACK IN THE FOLLY OF MY YOUTH

I WENT TO STAY WITH HER
TWO DAYS I LAY WITH HER
THEN I AWOKE TO THE ERROR OF MY WAYS

ANGEL & TESS

CAN I ATONE – CAN YOU FORGIVE ME
FOR WHAT WAS DONE WHILE STILL A CHILD?
SHOULD I STAY NUMB AND TAKE IT WITH ME?
WILL I BE LOVED AND NOT REVILED?

ALL OF THESE QUESTIONS DANCE BEFORE ME
HOW CAN I, THEN, SUPPRESS THE TRUTH
WHEN THESE TROUBLES, IN THEIR WAY
MADE ME WHO I AM TODAY?
THIS WAS THE FOLLY OF MY YOUTH

TESS Oh, Angel – I am almost glad – because now *you* can forgive *me*!

THOUGHT I WOULD REPEL YOU
IF I BROUGHT MYSELF TO TELL YOU
I HAD STRAYED

IF YOU WOULD LOVE ME – KNOW MY STORY
THIS IS THE COLD UNVARNISHED TRUTH
HOW I TRUSTED, AND I PAID
HAD MY INNOCENCE BETRAYED...

The lights fade.

End of Act I

ACT 2

Entr'acte.

Scene 1
The Same, Later That Night

ANGEL Tess, am I to believe this?

TESS In the name of our love, forgive me! I have forgiven you for the same.

ANGEL Yes – yes, you have.

TESS But you do not forgive me?

ANGEL Forgiveness does not apply to the case. You were one person; now you are another.

TESS I thought, Angel, that you loved me – me, my very self! Angel, I was a child – a child when it happened.

ANGEL You were more sinned against than sinning, that I admit. Tess! Say it is not true!

TESS It is true.

ANGEL Is he living?

TESS The baby died.

ANGEL But the man?

TESS He is alive.

ANGEL Is he in England?

TESS Yes.

    ANGEL *slumps, dejectedly.*

ANGEL Tess, let me speak plainly. How can we live together while that man lives, he being your husband in Nature, and not I? Think of years to come, and this past matter getting known – for it must get known.

TESS I suppose you are not going to live wi' me – long, are you, Angel?

ANGEL *exits as* **TESS** *weeps. She removes the jewellery and leaves it on the table.*

Scene 2
The Same *(Next Morning)*

ANGEL *&* **TESS** *prepare to leave.*

ANGEL Now, let us understand each other. There is no anger between us, though there is that which I cannot endure at present. I am thinking of going abroad for a time. They say that farmers may find easy independence in some parts of the world. Take this. It contains a good sum of money so that you should not want for anything while I am away.

TESS I agree to your conditions, Angel; because you know best what my punishment ought to be; only – don't make it more than I can bear!

ANGEL *turns and leaves without looking back.*

Scene 3
Multiple Locations

TESS *journeys home as the* **MAIDS** *become visible.* **IZZ** *tends to* **RETTY** *as* **MARIAN** *works in the fields.*

RETTY

GIVE ME YOUR LIPS
FOR MY HEART CALLS YOUR NAME
SHOW ME YOUR MERCY
SPARE ME THE SHAME

LONGING TO HOLD YOU
HOPING TO DRAW YOU NEAR
THEN – TO ENFOLD YOU
NOTHING TO FEAR

RETTY & IZZ

LOST IN THE VALE
WHERE THE LONG SHADOWS COMB
FIND ME BESIDE YOU
CARRY ME HOME

MARIAN & RETTY

GIVE ME YOUR LIPS
FOR MY HEART CALLS YOUR NAME
SHOW ME YOUR MERCY
SPARE ME THE SHAME

MARIAN, RETTY & IZZ

LONGING TO HOLD YOU
HOPING TO DRAW YOU NEAR
THEN – TO ENFOLD YOU
NOTHING TO FEAR

LOST IN THE VALE
WHERE THE LONG SHADOWS COMB
FIND ME BESIDE YOU
CARRY ME HOME

LOST IN THE VALE
WHERE THE LONG SHADOWS COMB
FIND ME BESIDE YOU
NOTHING DENIED YOU
HERE – LET ME GUIDE YOU
CARRY ME HOME

Scene 4
As Above, Except Tess, Who Arrives At
Her Parents' Cottage In Marlott

There follows a silent and shocked family reunion with **JOHN** *&*
JOAN.

MARIAN, RETTY & IZZ
CARRY ME HOME!

Scene 5
Durbeyfield Cottage

It is raining hard and the roof is leaking. **TESS**, *to one side, eavesdrops on the conversation.*

JOHN To think, now, that this be the end o't! I feel this too much, Joan; I shall put an end to myself, title and all – but she can make him keep her if he's married to her?

JOAN Why, yes. But she won't think o' doing that.

JOHN D'ye think he really have married her? – or is it like the first –

LISA-LU *enters.*

TESS I ought never to have come back here.

LISA LU You are going already?

TESS I can't stay here, Lisa Lu. Take this money – for the roof. Give it to Mother, mind...

Scene 6
The Parsonage At Emminster

ANGEL *with* **PARSON** *&* **MRS CLARE**.

MRS CLARE

WE THOUGHT IT BEST TO NOT ATTEND
THE WEDDING – LEAVE HER BE
TILL SHE HAS FOUND A WAY TO BLEND
IN WITH GENTILITY

PARSON CLARE

NOW YOU'VE NOT BROUGHT HER, AND YOU SAY
YOU'RE OFF AGAIN –

MRS CLARE

BUT STILL
I'M SURE YOU WON'T BE FAR AWAY?

ANGEL

I'M THINKING OF BRAZIL

MRS CLARE

ANGEL, YOU'RE JESTING!
I SEE THAT YOU'RE ON FORM
SAY SOMETHING, HUSBAND

PARSON CLARE

I HEAR IT'S RATHER WARM

ANGEL

MY WIFE'S AT HER MOTHER'S, WHERE SHE'LL STAY
UNTIL I'VE STAKED THE CLAIM
FRATERNISED WITH THE LOCAL PEOPLE

MRS CLARE *(Gasp)*

ROMAN CATHOLICS!

ANGEL

I HADN'T THOUGHT OF THAT

MRS CLARE

OH ANGEL, I MUST DISAGREE

WILL WE NOT GET TO MEET YOUR WIFE

BEFORE YOU PUT TO SEA?

SURELY, SHE'S PRETTY?
HER MAIDEN CHEEKS AGLOW

MR CLARE

YOU WERE HER FIRST LOVE?

ANGEL

I'D LIKE TO THINK IT'S SO...

Scene 7
A Mountainside Farm

The **LABOURERS** *work at swede-hacking.* **MARIAN**, *who is among them, occasionally takes a sly drink.*

ENSEMBLE
> AND THE LORD SAID –
> AND THE LORD SAID –
> AND THE LORD SAID –
> AND THE LORD SAID –
>
> THAT THE SEED THAT HAS FALLEN ON STONY GROUND SHALL NOT
>   PREVAIL IN THE END
> THAT THE THORN AND GORSEBUSH WILL SMOTHER EACH SHOOT –
>   SEE IT WITHER AND BEND
> THAT THE LAND WILL BE BARREN SO UNRIGHTEOUS MEN SHALL
>   HAVE NOTHING TO TEND

MARIAN
> OH, MY LORD, I'M CALLING TO YOU
> WITNESS OUR DESPAIR
> HERE WE TILL THE MOUNTAIN
> STARVED OF AIR
> WE ARE SINNERS ALL
> AND KNOW OUR PENANCE MUST BE PAID
> TILL YOUR PERFECT MERCY
> IS DISPLAYED

ENSEMBLE
> AND THE LORD SAID –
> AND THE LORD SAID –
> AND THE LORD SAID –
> AND THE LORD SAID –
>
> THAT THE SEED THAT HAS FALLEN ON STONY GROUND IS NOT A
>   PART OF HIS PLAN
> THAT THE SEED THAT IS CHOKED BY THE THORNBUSH WILL WITHER
>   FROM WHENCE IT BEGAN
> THAT THE LAND WILL BE BARREN UNTIL FAITH TAKES ROOT IN THE
>   HEART OF EACH MAN

TESS *enters.*

MARIAN Tess – Mrs Clare – the wife of dear he!

TESS *(as they embrace)* Marian, dear Marian! Will you do me a good turn without asking questions? My husband has gone abroad, and I have overrun my allowance, so that I have to fall back upon my old work for a time. Do they want a hand here?

MARIAN Oh yes; they'll take one always, because so few care to come. 'Tis a starve-acre place. Corn and swedes are all they grow. If you engage, you'll be swede-hacking. That's what I am doing; but you won't like it.

TESS Very well. Now, Marian, remember – nothing about *him*, if I get the place. I don't wish to bring his name down to the dirt.

MARIAN But you be a gentleman's wife; and it hardly seems fair that you should live like this!

TESS I ought to have sent him a letter. He said I could not go to him, but he didn't say I was not able to write. I will go to his family at Emminster this Sunday coming.

Scene 8
The Church At Emminster *(The Following Sunday)*

PARSON *&* **MRS CLARE** *and the congregation sing a dirge of a hymn.*

ENSEMBLE
> JOYFULLY, WE PRAISE
> JOYFULLY, WE SING
> TO THE GOD OF AGES PAST
> TO THE SHEPHERD KING
>
> HE WHO ROSE AGAIN
> TO SAVE US ALL FROM SIN
> NOW, HIS FAITHFUL SERVANTS
> INVITE THEIR MASTER IN

A preacher rises to the pulpit. He turns – it is **ALEC**.

ALEC And God spoke these words, saying: "Thou shalt have no other Gods before me. Thou shalt not make unto thee any graven image, or any likeness of any thing that is in heaven above, or that is in the earth beneath. Thou shalt not kill. Thou shalt not commit –"

TESS *enters and* **ALEC** *freezes as he sees her. The congregation, including the* **CLARES**, *turns to look at her.* **TESS** *runs.*

Scene 9
The Road From Emminster

TESS *attempts to get away.*

ALEC *(from off)* Tess!

She slows. **ALEC** *enters.*

Tess! It is I – Alec D'Urberville.

TESS I see it is.

ALEC Your sudden appearance unnerved me in there. But God helped me through it. And immediately afterwards I felt that, of all the persons in the world whom it was my duty and desire to save from the wrath to come, the woman whom I had so grievously wronged was that person. If you could only know, Tess, the sense of security, the certainty –

TESS Don't go on with it! You, and those like you, take your fill of pleasure on earth by making the life of such as me bitter and black with sorrow; and then it is a fine thing, when you have had enough of that, to think of securing your place in heaven by becoming converted!

ALEC I never took you for a sceptic. I'm sorry you are not a believer.

TESS I have learned many things in my troubles.

ALEC What troubles have you had?

TESS

I HAD A SON – HE ARRIVED WITH THE SPRING
SUCH A FRAGILE AND TENDER CHILD
ONE AMONG MANY
BORN TEN-A-PENNY
WISE TO REJECT THE LIFE I GAVE HIM

TELL ME, IF YOU WERE HIS FATHER
WOULD YOU HAVE DEIGNED TO PAY?
BROUGHT HIM THE BEST, OR RATHER
HAVE TURNED US BOTH AWAY?

I HAD A CHILD – SUCH A MEEK LITTLE THING
WITH A MOTHER UNCLEAN, DEFILED
NO AIRS OR GRACES

NO SACRED PLACE IS
KEPT FOR HER BOY – THEY WOULD NOT SAVE HIM

I HAD A CHILD WHO HAD NO HOME TO CLAIM
SO THEN "SORROW" BECAME HIS NAME

ALEC

YOU HAD A SON – SO THEN, I HAD A CHILD
YET YOU WOULD NOT APPROACH MY DOOR
I COULD HAVE PROFFERED
LODGINGS – HAVE OFFERED
MEDICINE AND DOCTORS – DON'T YOU KNOW ME?

TESS

YOU WOULD HAVE ADDED
    CONDITIONS
LIKE OTHER PLOTS YOU'VE
    HATCHED
I KNEW THOSE FINE PHYSICIANS
WOULD COME WITH STRINGS
    ATTACHED

	ALEC

I HAD A SON – I AM NOW
    RECONCILED
WITH MY PAST, THOUGH THE
    WOUNDS ARE RAW
CONQUER EMOTION
CLING TO THE NOTION
I CAN ESCAPE THE HELLS
    BELOW ME
	I HAD A SON – I AM NOW
	    RECONCILED
	WITH MY PAST, THOUGH THE
	    WOUNDS ARE RAW
	THROUGH MY DEVOTION
	TRUST IN THE NOTION
	I CAN ESCAPE THE HELLS
	    BELOW ME

I HAD A SON WHO WAS BORN
    INTO SHAME
AND MY SORROW BECAME HIS
    NAME
	YOU HAD A SON WHO WAS
	    BORN INTO SHAME
	AND YOUR SORROW BECAME
	    HIS NAME

ALEC Don't look at me like that.

TESS I beg your pardon?

ALEC No, don't beg my pardon. Well – you will see me again.

TESS No. Do not come near me!

ALEC I will think. But, Tess, swear before we part, that you will never tempt me again – by your charms or your ways.

TESS Good God – how can you ask what is so unnecessary!

ALEC And since you wear a veil to hide your good looks, why don't you keep it down? Women's faces have had too much power over me already for me not to fear them!

TESS *covers her face.*

Scene 10
The Mountainside Farm

TESS *and the* LABOURERS *at the steam thresher. During the song,* ALEC *enters and looks on.*

ENSEMBLE
> INTO THE BELLY OF THE BEAST
> FEED EVERY VESTIGE OF THE CORN

MEN
> WE MUST PROVIDE AN ENDLESS FEAST
> NATURE DEVOURED WITH SENSELESS SCORN
>
> INTO THE THRESHER, FEED YOUR SOUL
> STEAM WILL DECIDE ITS FINAL FATE

WOMEN
> ONE WHIRRING DRUM PERFORMS YOUR ROLE
> JUMP TO THE TASK – IT WILL NOT WAIT

MEN
> INTO A TRAP – A DOUBLE-BIND

WOMEN
> SLAVES TO THE TYRANT OF THE FLAME

MEN
> NOW THAT WE'RE BROKEN MEN –

ALL
> YOU'LL FIND US TAME

> *Sound effects – whistle. The* LABOURERS *step away from the machine.*

MAN *(noticing* ALEC*)* Who is that?

WOMAN Somebody's fancy-man, I s'pose.

MARIAN *(to* TESS*)* You ought to get a quart o' drink into 'ee, as I've done. You wouldn't look so white then.

> ALEC *approaches* TESS.

TESS You have refused my last request, not to come near me!

ALEC Yes, but I have a good reason. Will you put it in my power to make the only reparation I can for the wrong I did you: that is, will you be my wife?

TESS O no, sir – no!

ALEC Why is that?

TESS There is...someone else...

ALEC Someone else... But has not a sense of what is morally right and proper any weight with you?

TESS I have married him.

ALEC Is he on this farm?

TESS He is far away.

ALEC Far away? From you? What sort of a husband can he be?

TESS O, do not speak against him! It was through you. He found out!

LISA LU *enters.*

LISA LU Tess!

TESS Liza-Lu!

LISA LU I have been traipsing about all day, Tess, a trying to find 'e. 'Tis father. He just dropped down. It were his heart. The doctor said there were no chance for him.

TESS Father? O, Father!

Scene 11
The Durbeyfield Cottage

JOAN, TESS & LISA-LU *are visited by their* LANDLORD.

LANDLORD It be no use arguin'. The house is in the name o' yer late husband and ye hae no further right to bide.

JOAN But we can pay – as weekly tenants!

LANDLORD Not wi' she 'ere.

JOAN Who? Tess?

LANDLORD She is not – a proper woman.

JOAN *(as the* LANDLORD *retreats)* Damn ye to hell! May yer dirty soul be burnt into cinders!

The LANDLORD *exits.* LISA-LU *exits after him.*

TESS

UNTIL MY HEART IS FREE
AND UNTIL MY DYING DAY
MY LIFE IS NOT MY OWN
THE PAST IS HERE TO STAY

HOW CAN YOU HOLD ME
TO YOUR ETERNAL PLAN
WHEN NO-ONE TOLD ME

JOAN

TILL THEY WOULD SCOLD THEE –

BOTH

WHAT IS MAN!

TESS

UNTIL MY HEART IS FREE
OF YOUR COLD INHUMAN CREED
UPON THIS BLIGHTED EARTH
I BEG AND SCRAPE AND BLEED...

Scene 12
Outside The Durbeyfield Cottage

TESS and **LISA LU** *are packing, in readiness to leave.* **ALEC** *sidles up, dressed in his old attire.* **TESS** *gestures* **LISA LU** *away.*

ALEC Where are you going?

TESS Kingsbere.

ALEC *snorts, derisively.*

Mother is so foolish about Father's people that she will go there.

ALEC Why not come to Trantridge? You can all live there quite comfortably. I owe you something for the past, you know. And you cured me, too, of that religious craze.

TESS You have given up your preaching entirely?

ALEC Tess, I was on the way to salvation till I saw you again! Here I am, my love, as in the old times!

COME AWAY
TAKE MY HAND
YOU OF ALL GIRLS, MY DEAR, SHOULD UNDERSTAND

WHAT ARE THESE
TIES THAT BIND?
LEAVE THAT MULE YOU CALL HUSBAND FAR BEHIND!

I KNOW YOU LIKE FORBIDDEN FRUIT
SHOW ME YOUR APPETITE'S UNABATED
AND PUT AN END TO MY PURSUIT
I CAN ENSURE THAT YOUR HUNGER'S SATED...

TESS slaps ALEC. ALEC grabs TESS, as if he is about to strike her.

TESS

STRIKE ME AND PUNISH ME – FOR I KNOW THE LAW
ONCE VICTIM, ALWAYS VICTIM – YOURS, EVERMORE!

*TESS breaks free of **ALEC**'s grasp and exits.*

Scene 13
A Street In Kingsbere *(Evening)*

JOAN, LISA-LU *&* TESS *arrive with their luggage.*

JOAN Well, children, welcome to Kingsbere. Where lie those ancestors whom yer father spoke of and sung to painfulness.

MAN *(entering, with a lantern)* You be the woman they call Mrs D'Urberville?

JOAN Widow of the late Sir John D'Urberville and returning to the domain of my knight's forefathers.

MAN Oh? Well, I know nothing about that; but if you be Mrs D'Urberville, I am sent to tell 'ee that the rooms you wanted be let. We didn't know you was coming till we got your letter this morning – when 'twas too late. No doubt you can get other lodgings elsewhere.

The MAN *exits.*

JOAN Well, 'ere's a welcome to your ancestors' lands! But isn't our family vault our own freehold? Why of course 'tis, and that's where we will camp, till the place of our ancestors finds us a roof!

Scene 14
Outside The D'Urberville Vaults *(Later That Evening)*

The **ENSEMBLE** *enter and stand frozen in place, as if statues.*
JOAN *and* **LISA-LU** *retire into the shadows.*

OFFSTAGE VOICES

OO...

TESS *approaches a barred door.*

TESS Why am I on the wrong side of this door?

Scene 15
Interior Of The D'Urberville Vaults
(Immediately Afterwards)

TESS *enters the vaults and examines the statues. As she does so, one of the "statues" moves – it is* **ALEC***. She starts.*

ALEC I saw you come in, and would not interrupt your meditations. A family gathering, is it not, with these old fellows beneath us? *(Stamps foot)* And you thought I was the mere stone reproduction of one of them. But no. The old order changeth. The little finger of the sham D'Urberville can do more for you now than the whole dynasty of the real underneath...

The statues move to reflect changes in perspective as **ALEC** *pursues* **TESS** *through the vaults.*

	ENSEMBLE
MAKE YOUR DECISION	AH...
LOOK TO YOUR FOREBEARS	
THIS IS BY DESIGN	
TO REINSTATE THEIR LINE	
DO YOU WASTE AWAY ON PIOUS NOTIONS	
JOIN THEM AS A NOBLE WRAITH?	
OR DO YOU RELENT AND SERVE YOUR FAMILY	
THROW AWAY INJURIOUS FAITH?	

	TESS
MAKE YOUR DECISION	MAKE YOUR DECISION
LOOK TO YOUR MOTHER	LOOK AT YOUR MOTHER
YOU ALONE CAN SAVE	YOU ALONE CAN SAVE
HER FROM AN EARLY GRAVE	HER FROM A PAUPER'S GRAVE
WHAT ABOUT YOUR SISTER – SEE HER SUFFERING	
DOES SHE KNOW THE POWER YOU HOLD	
TO RESTORE THEIR HOUSE TO FORMER GLORY?	
FETED AS IN DAYS OF OLD	

TESS

HOW DO I RESIST YOU WHEN
    YOU TANGLE UP MY
    THOUGHTS?
WHISPERING THE WORDS I
    WANT TO HEAR

PLAY ON MY EMOTIONS – SO
    DISTORTED, OUT OF SORTS   **ALEC**
IT'S YOU WHO I SHOULD FEAR   THIS – THE BOLD VENEER

BOTH

I HEAR YOUR VOICE – IT TWISTS AGAIN INSIDE OF ME
AND I FEEL YOUR HEAT AS YOU DRAW NEAR
FOR, IF THE GATES OF HEAVEN ARE DENIED TO ME
I MUST ENDURE CORRUPTION HERE

ALEC   **TESS**

I HEAR YOUR VOICE – IT TWISTS   I HEAR YOUR VOICE…
    AGAIN INSIDE OF ME
AND I FEEL YOUR BREATH AS   I FEEL YOUR BREATH…
    YOU DRAW NEAR

BOTH

IF I SHOULD TRUST YOU – WOULD I FIND YOU'D LIED TO ME?
WANTING TO TAKE ALL I HOLD DEAR

I WANT TO TASTE A WORLD WHICH WAS DENIED TO ME

TESS

FREE FROM DESTRUCTION, FREE
    FROM FEAR   **ALEC**
                                   SAY THE WORD, MY DEAR
END THEIR SUFFERING HERE…

They embrace.

Scene 16
The Parsonage At Emminster

A sick and pallid looking ANGEL *stands D.S. as* PARSON *&* MRS
CLARE *look on in horror.*

MRS CLARE O, it is not Angel – not my son – the Angel who went
away!

ANGEL I was ill over there, you know. I am all right now. Most of
the Europeans who were with me suffered and wasted away.
I have seen... Has any letter come for me lately?

PARSON CLARE *(retrieving the letter for* ANGEL*)* Only the one...

Scene 17
Split Scene: As Above/The Mountainside Farm

ANGEL *reads the letter as* MARIAN *appears.*

MARIAN Honoured Sir – Look to your wife if you do love her as much as she do love you. For she is sore put to by an enemy in the shape of a friend: in short, sir, a young squire from Trantridge by the name of Alec D'Urberville.

Scene 18
The Journey To Trantridge

ANGEL *makes his way to Trantridge.*

Scene 19
Trantridge

LISA LU *shows* ANGEL *in.* JOAN *enters.*

ANGEL Mrs Durbeyfield. My name is Angel Clare. I am – Tess's husband.

JOAN She don't live here.

ANGEL Do you know if she is well?

JOAN I don't. But you ought to, sir.

ANGEL Do you think Tess would wish me to try and find her?

JOAN I don't think she would.

ANGEL *turns to leave.*

ANGEL Are you in want of anything?

JOAN No, sir. As you can see, we are quite well provided for.

LISA-LU She is in Sandbourne.

ANGEL Where there?

JOAN *hands him an envelope by way of reply.*

A boarding-house?

He folds the envelope.

Thank you!

Scene 20
The Journey To Sandbourne

ANGEL *makes his way through the resort as holidaymakers enjoy the sea air.*

Scene 21
A Boarding-House In Sandbourne

A **LANDLADY** *appears.*

ANGEL Is there a Mrs Clare lodging here?

LANDLADY No, sir. Nobody by that name.

ANGEL Then how about Durbeyfield? Miss Theresa Durbeyfield.

LANDLADY There is a Mrs D'Urberville, sir.

ANGEL Will you kindly tell her that a relative is anxious to see her?

LANDLADY What name shall I give, sir?

ANGEL
Angel.

> *The* **LANDLADY** *exits.* **ANGEL** *paces anxiously.* **TESS** *enters, dressed in finery.* **ANGEL** *turns and sees her. A moment passes before he can bring himself to speak.*

How did you get to be – like this? Can you forgive me? Can't you – come to me?

TESS Don't come close to me, Angel!

ANGEL Don't you love me, because I have been so pulled down by illness?

TESS
ONCE, I WAS YOURS
BUT YOUR MORALS WERE HARSH, UNBENDING
TREMULOUS IN
MY ORIGINAL SIN

YES, YOU HAD CAUSE
BUT THE PENALTY SEEMED UNENDING
THEN, LIKE A GHOST
CAME THE ONE I FEARED MOST

LYING AND PERSUADING
TILL HIS NOTIONS, SO DEGRADING
SEEMED THE ONLY MEANS OF AIDING
THOSE AROUND ME

ONCE, I WAS YOURS
NOW THERE'S NO POINT IN US PRETENDING
I CAN BE SAVED
SOILED AND DEPRAVED   **ANGEL**
                               PLEASE FORGIVE ME
WHAT WAS MY CRIME –   I HAVE SEEN THE DARKNESS
TO BE DAMNED FOR ALL TIME?   LOST IN A WORLD WITHOUT
                                   LOVE
                               STARING INTO THE FINAL ABYSS

I LIE DESECRATING
EVERY SACRED VOW, CREATING   NOW I KNOW WHAT IS TRUE
MY OWN GALLOWS – AND I'M   FOR BEWILDERMENT GREW
    HATING
EVERY MOMENT   EVERY MOMENT I SPENT
                               WITHOUT YOU –

ONCE, I WAS YOURS   – MY LOVE...
AND IT'S YOUR NAME THAT I'M
    DEFENDING
NO-ONE NEED KNOW
HOW I'M LAID LOW

I'VE MADE MY BED, SIR
THAT'S TAKEN AS READ, SIR
YOUR LOVER IS DEAD, SIR
NOW GO!

GO!

TESS *turns and exits.* **ANGEL** *stands, stunned, for a moment before he too exits. A row ensues, off, between* **ALEC** *and* **TESS**. *The* **LANDLADY** *enters, listening to the commotion.*

(off)
YOU BROKE MY HEART
YOU BULLIED ME AND LIED TO
    ME   **ALEC** *(off)*
AND TOLD ME   COME BACK TO BED, MY DEAR
HE NEVER WOULD RETURN   SEEMS AS THOUGH YOU'RE
                               CONFUSED AGAIN
YET, THERE HE STOOD   THE MAN YOU LOVED
AND SOMETHING TORE INSIDE   MIGHT AS WELL BE DEAD, MY
    OF ME   DEAR
I FEEL MY SHAME   COME LIE WITH ME, INSTEAD

AND ANGER BURN

I COULD NEVER
LOVE YOU

AFTER WHAT YOU'VE DONE

TO ME...

UNTIL MY HEART IS

FREE
I MUST JOURNEY ON
JOURNEY ON...

FOR YOU LIED TO ME, LIED TO
    ME
LIED TO ME, LIED TO ME
LIED TO ME!

YOU'LL FEEL BETTER THEN
LET US TASTE FORBIDDEN
    FRUIT...

THIS IS THE WOMAN WHO
    CARRIED MY CHILD
IT'S A LITTLE TOO LATE FOR
    THAT...
LOOK AT ME
LITTLE WHORE!
YOU ARE MINE
NOTHING LESS AND NOTHING
    MORE
MAKE YOUR DECISION
THINK OF YOUR MOTHER
GET UNDRESSED, COME OVER
    HERE
OR I'LL SEND YOU BACK, MY
    DEAR
MOTHER WILL BE HOMELESS
SISTER WILL HAVE TO BEG!

The row concludes with a loud crashing noise and a screeching orchestral dischord. A door slams, off. Onstage, the **LANDLADY** *looks on as* **TESS** *hurriedly crosses the stage in front of her.*

Scene 22
The Landing Outside Alec's Room

The **LANDLADY** *knocks on* **ALEC***'s door. There is no response.*

LANDLADY Mr D'Urberville.

She opens the door, sees **ALEC***'s body, and screams. SFX – police whistles, and then whistling from, and the sound of, a steam locomotive.*

Scene 23
Sandborne Railway Station

ANGEL *stands dejectedly with his suitcase.* TESS *runs in.*

TESS *(breathless)* I saw you – I saw you make the turn for the station and I have been following you all this way!

ANGEL Thank God! Tess, what is that on your hands?

TESS Angel, do you know what I have been running after you for? To tell you that I have killed him!

ANGEL What?

TESS I have done it – I don't know how. Angel, I thought as I ran along that you would be sure to forgive me now that I have done that. I was unable to bear your not loving me. Say you do now, dear, dear husband; say you do, now I have killed him!

ANGEL I do love you, Tess – O, I do. I will not desert you, whatever you may or may not have done! We must leave at once. Can you walk well, Tessy?

TESS I feel strong enough to walk any distance!

ANGEL *leads* TESS *away.*

Scene 24
Outside A Manor House *(Evening)*

ANGEL *&* TESS *enter.*

ANGEL I know this place. It is Bramhurst manor house. You can see that it is shut up, and grass is growing on the drive.

TESS All those rooms empty, and we without a roof to our heads!

ANGEL You are getting tired, Tessy. Come, let us see if we can't climb inside…

Scene 25
Manor Interior

TESS *and* ANGEL *at rest inside the house.*

ANGEL Rest at last!

TESS All is trouble outside there; inside here content.

ANGEL We'll leave here tomorrow night.

TESS Why should we put an end to all that's sweet and lovely!

> DON'T THINK OF OUTSIDE THESE ROOMS
> NOW ISN'T OVER
> DON'T SEE HOW TOMORROW LOOMS ONCE MORE
> MADNESS MAY DESCEND
> TURN OUR FEVERED THOUGHTS TO FRENZY
> NOW ISN'T OVER
> NOW ISN'T OVER

ANGEL

> DESOLATE WITHOUT YOU
> CAME TO SEE THE GOOD
> NOW EVERYTHING ABOUT YOU
> SPEAKS OF NOBLE BLOOD

BOTH

> DON'T THINK OF OUTSIDE THESE ROOMS
> NOW ISN'T OVER
> DON'T DWELL ON THOSE GHOSTLY TOMBS OF YORE
> NOT THINGS DONE, BUT WILLED

ANGEL   TESS

> NOT THE ACT, BUT YOUR   NOT THE ACT, BUT YOUR
>   VOLITION   CONTRITION

BOTH

> NOW ISN'T OVER
> NOW ISN'T OVER

They embrace.

> NOW ISN'T FLEETING
> THE HEART ISN'T BEATING

TESS

DON'T THINK OF OUTSIDE THESE ROOMS

ANGEL
DON'T DWELL ON THOSE GHOSTLY TOMBS

BOTH
DON'T SEE HOW TOMORROW LOOMS
ONCE MORE

Scene 26
Stonehenge *(Night)*

ANGEL *&* TESS *approach Stonehenge under cover of darkness. Sound effects – the wind makes a peculiar humming noise as it blows between the stones [synth pad].*

ANGEL What monstrous place is this...? It is Stonehenge!

TESS The heathen temple?

ANGEL Older than the centuries; older than the D'Urbervilles! Well, what shall we do? We may find shelter Father on.

TESS Can't we rest here?

ANGEL I fear not. This spot is visible for miles by day. *(Beat)* I think you are lying on an altar.

TESS It seems as if there were no folk in the world but we two; and I wish there were not – except 'Liza-Lu. Angel, if anything happens to me, will you watch over 'Liza Lu for my sake? She is so good and pure. O, Angel – I wish you would marry her if you lose me, as you will do shortly.

ANGEL If I lose you I lose all!

TESS Did they make sacrifices here?

ANGEL Yes.

TESS Who to?

ANGEL I believe to the sun.

TESS Tell me, Angel, do you think we shall meet again after we are dead?

He kisses her.

O, Angel – I fear that means no! And I wanted to see you again – so very much!

OFFSTAGE VOICES
OO...

Music. TESS *falls asleep – time passes.*

ANGEL *stands guard until he, too, succumbs to tiredness.*

Scene 27
The Same *(Dawn)*

The lighting changes as the sun rises. ANGEL *sleeps at* TESS*'s feet. He is awoken by a* POLICEMAN *approaching.* ANGEL *leaps to his feet and reaches for a weapon.*

POLICEMAN   *(stopping)* It is no use, sir. There are sixteen of us on the Plain, and the whole county is up in arms.

TESS   *(waking)* Have they come for me?

ANGEL   Yes, they have come.

TESS   Angel, I am almost glad. This happiness could not have lasted. And now I shall not live for you to despise me!

TESS *stands.*

I am ready.

Scene 28
A Lane And The Fields Around Stonehenge

TESS *is led away as the* **ENSEMBLE** *tends the surrounding fields.*

ENSEMBLE

THE FIELDS HAVE BEEN OPENED
THE DOG-DAYS ARE HERE
THE HEIGHT OF THE SUMMER
WILL SOON DISAPPEAR
WITH HARVEST UPON US
IT'S TIME WE EARN OUR KEEP
THE GOOD SEED HAS BEEN GROWING
AND WHAT WE SOW, WE REAP

MEN

CAST YOUR EYES UNTO THE
    GROUND

NO EVIL DO WE SEE
SAD WHEN ALL THE FATES
    CONFOUND
A MAID AS FAIR AS SHE

WOMEN

NO EVIL DO WE SEE

A MAID AS FAIR AS SHE…

Scene 29
Journey To The City

The **ENSEMBLE** *gradually down their farming tools and set to work with factory machinery, signifying migration to the city.*

ALL

INTO THE BELLY OF THE BEAST
FEED EVERY VESTIGE OF THE CORN

WE MUST PROVIDE AN ENDLESS FEAST
NATURE DEVOURED WITH SENSELESS SCORN

MEN

INTO A TRAP – A DOUBLE-BIND

WOMEN

SLAVES TO THE TYRANT OF THE FLAME

MEN

NOW THAT WE'RE BROKEN MEN –

ALL

YOU'LL FIND US TAME

Scene 30
Winchester Gaol

TESS *enters as the* **ENSEMBLE** *look on. She is led towards the gallows.*

ENSEMBLE

AND THE LORD SAID –
AND THE LORD SAID –
AND THE LORD SAID –
AND THE LORD SAID –

THAT THE SEED THAT HAS FALLEN ON STONY GROUND SHALL NOT
    PREVAIL IN THE END
THAT THE THORN AND GORSEBUSH WILL SMOTHER EACH SHOOT…
    (Etc)

On the final drum beat **TESS** *bows her head and freezes. Beat. The scene transforms to the country road outside of Marlott.*

Scene 31
The Road Outside Marlott

JOHN DURBEYFIELD *enters, drunk, as* **PARSON TRINGHAM**
crosses.

JOHN

GOOD NIGHT T'YE, PARSON

PARSON

GOOD EVENING, SIR JOHN

JOHN *starts, as if to ask the* **PARSON** *a question, but then notices
the flagon of ale in his hands. He shrugs and takes a drink
instead.* **JOHN** *and the* **PARSON** *exit.*

Scene 32
Dance On The Village Green

The young **FEMALE ENSEMBLE** *becomes prominent, dancing in their ceremonial white dresses. They approach* **TESS**.

GIRLS
CHILDREN OF THE EARTH AND CHILDREN OF THE SUN *(Etc)*

CHILDREN OF THE EARTH
COME SING AND DANCE – AND JOIN WITH ME
WELCOME THE SUMMER
BATHE IN THE LIGHT
WORSHIP GODS OF OLD TONIGHT

GIRLS & TESS
CHILDREN OF THE EARTH AND CHILDREN OF THE SUN *(Etc)*

TESS
CHILDREN OF THE EARTH AND CHILDREN OF THE STARS...

ANGEL *enters and dances with the* **GIRLS** *before coming face-to-face with* **TESS**. *The rest of the* **ENSEMBLE** *enters as onlookers.*

SAY, WON'T YOU STAY, SIR, AND DANCE WITH US TILL MORNING?

ANGEL *takes* **TESS** *in his arms.*

I KNOW HOW IT FEELS...   **ANGEL**
                                THOSE WHEELS WITHIN
                                      WHEELS

BOTH
I DEAL IN IDEALS

ENSEMBLE *(as* **TESS** *and* **ANGEL** *embrace)*
CHILDREN OF THE EARTH AND CHILDREN OF THE SOIL
CHILDREN OF THE EARTH AND CHILDREN OF THE SUN

CHILDREN OF THE EARTH!

The End

Furniture and List

In the original production the action took place against a composite set which suggested ancient and partially derelict stone edifices, enabling the representation of not only Stonehenge but cottages and ancient mansions when co-ordinated with effective lighting. Within the 'stonework' were a number of points of ingress and egress. 'Depth' was created by the addition of accoutrements symbolic of Victorian country life such as bales of hay, with many props preset in plain view of the audience. A number of portable wooden blocks were used to form 'furniture' and the stone slab on which Tess rests at Stonehenge. Some props were mimed, or signified by an actor-musician's instrument. To what extent the mis-en-scene is embodied by the actors, as opposed to literally represented, is the prerogative of individual creative teams. Below is a list of props which may be helpful in the realisation of the work:

Act 1

Egg basket (p.1)

Flagon for John (p.1)

Tankards (p.7)

Strawberries (p.10)

Letter (p.12)

Birdcage (p.15)

Druggist's bottle (p.22)

Baby* (p.27)

Jug of water (p.28)

Basket (p.31)

Milking stools (p.32)

Book/s (p.36)

Bag containing black pudding and a bottle of mead (p.42)

Gift box containing necklace (p.57)

Suitcases (p.57)

Act 2

Suitcase for Angel (p.62)

Flask / bottle for Marian (p.69)

Bible for Alec (p.71)

Lantern (p.79)

Letter (p.83)

Envelope (p.86)

Flagon (p.102)

*ultimately mimed in the original production

Sound Effects

In the original production many sound effects were generated by the actor-musicians or by synthesiser.

Act 1

Sound of horse's hooves travelling at varying speeds* (p.13)

Birds whistling* (p.15)

Baby crying, rising to a crescendo (p.28)

Steam train standing (p.50)

Steam train whistling and departing (p.50)

Wedding bells* (p.55)

Act 2

Rain and leaking roof (p.66)

Steam thresher (p.75)

Steam whistle (p.75)

Add reverb to voxes, etc. in vaults (p.80 – 82)

Crashing noise and door slamming, off* (p.90)

Police whistles and steam train whistling (p.91)

Steam train/s at railway station (p.92)

Wind blowing between the stones at Stonehenge* (p.96)

* sound effect generated by cast / band in original production

Lighting

Effective lighting was a vital component of the original production, owing to the rapid cinematic-style transitions required between scenes on a composite set. The lighting was expressionistic and, therefore, as suggestive of inner emotional states as of external realities. Blackouts were used sparingly with scenes transitioning via cross-fades where practicable. Smoke was used during the railway sequences, and to signify mist (eg during the rape scene).

Lighting and effects

Earthy colours; expressionistic – mood most important; very fluid.

Act 1

Preset
Suggestion of Stonehenge – arches visible, rest cool. Needs to be bright enough to allow people to see their way to the bar by crossing up and down the stage.

b/o   cue: clearance
Overture   Brooding

Pg1   Crossroads
Late May evening, warm and pleasant
Cue: end of overture.

Pg1   Fate
Darkening/intensifying of crossroads. Anticipation of life-changing event.
Cue: "Good evening, Sir John"

Pg2   Fate 2
Continuation of above i.e. greater darkening/intensity
Cue: "What the records show?"

Pg3   Village Green
Later the same evening, warm, rich, earthy and welcoming
– a pagan fertility ritual
Cue: "...bones in his family plot!"

Pg6   Dance
Heavily stylised (side-lit?), deep, deep feeling – as if nothing in the
world exists but the dancers and their moving bodies, sensual and
extremely intense.
Cue: "Ah, 'tis only in fun, Tess."

Pg6   Village Green
As above
Cue: "Come along, Angel, or it will be dark before we get to
Emminster."

Pg6   I Saw Your Face
Focus on Tess. Ethereal – we are inside her head.
Cue: Angel exits

Pg7   Rolliver's Inn
Night/no natural light, dimly lit, full of alcoholic vapours,
claustrophobic but fairly warm and jolly
Cue: "Those lives changed by a word, a deed"

Pg10   Trantridge exterior
Daytime, artificial Garden of Eden, would be beautiful but nothing is
quite right
Cue: "...leave it to me about asking for help."

Pg12   Cottage interior
Daytime, working class home, somewhat hard and dour, some natural light
Cue: "Offers a world that can get… exciting"

Pg13   Gig
Daytime, Tess and Alec on a gig DC, edgy and dangerous
Cue: "It is no other kind of opportunity."

Pg14   Trantridge exterior
As above
Cue: "My life upon it!"

Pg15   Trantridge interior
Daytime, gaudy opulence – drawing room of the wealthy but tasteless
Cue: "…an old lady, and blind."

Pg16   Trantridge exterior
As above
Cue: "The servants will show you around."

Pg17   Chaseborough
Night, interior of a large room in a grimy and unpleasant inn, a 19th century "nightclub" where people go to get as intoxicated as possible – wild and threatening feeling
Cue: Tess and Alec finish whistling

P20   Chaseborough
Night, exterior of the inn
Cue: "Sing it again…"

Pg21   Wood
Autumn night, moonlit, fairy tale-esque, dark and mysterious
Cue: "Out of the frying-pan into the fire!"

Pg22   Hallucination
As above but increasingly distorted and surreal as drugs take effect on
Tess
Cue: Tess drinks from the bottle

Pg22   Rape
Very shadowy and grotesque
Cue: "So I have brought my lover -"

Pg23   Country Lane
Autumn morning, bleak, depressing and cold
Cue: Tess rises

Pg25   Cottage exterior
Same autumn morning as above
Cue: Joan enters

Pg26   Village Green
As above but wistful and melancholic
Cue: Girls enter

Pg27   Dog-Days
Daytime, a field in deepest hottest summer
Cue: "Come and share the evening, fancy-free!"

Pg28   Cottage interior
Night, some fairly feeble lamp/candle/fire light
Cue: "Lay claim to heart and soul"

Pg28   b/o
Slow as the baby crying sfx cuts out.
Cue: "Amen."

Pg29   Chapel
Morning, austere, cold and stark
Cue: leave a slight pause after the baby sfx stops

Pg30   Graveside
Gloomy afternoon, oppressive, foreboding
Cue: "It will be just the same."

Pg31   Country Lane
Spring dawn, faintly lit, with shadows
Cue: "That's how the spirit dies!"

Pg32   Dairy exterior
Warm and welcoming spring day, a rural idyll, tranquil, everything in harmony
Cue: "All until my heart is free!"

Pg36   Dairy (later)
As above but evening
Cue:"and that's saying a good deal."

Pg37   Dairy (transition)   as above but sense of season
progressing through to a perfect beautiful warm summer
Cue: "I deal in ideals" (before "Interlude as TESS draws close to ANGEL")

P38   Dairy interior & exterior
A summer morning – split scene
Cue: Final "I deal in ideals"

Pg38   Will you marry me?
Somewhat surreal version of Dairy as we go into girls' heads
Cue: "And I!"

Pg40   Dairy
Interior summer
Cue: "He'll not marry thee!"

Pg42   Parsonage exterior
Summer day, less beautiful than dairy, perhaps a sense of being cloudy overhead
Cue: "But he is sure to marry her."

Pg43   Parsonage interior
Middle-class household, good amount of natural light, everything clean and crisp
Cue: Cuthbert and Felix enter

Pg45   Parsonage interior (later)   as above but evening, perhaps some artificial light
Cue: "Hmm…"

Pg47   Race back to the Dairy
Country Lane, summer
Cue: "ALL: A truly Christian woman who's virtuous and pure"

Pg48   Dairy exterior
As above
Cue: Tess onstage skimming milk

Pg50   Railway Station
Summer evening, heavily stylised - dark and foreboding like the underworld, with the garish bright light of the steam train's lantern, smoke machine
Cue: "- when we take the milk to the station"

Pg50   Train departing
"Train" leaves DS, lighting becomes more naturalistic but still a little foreboding
Cue: "It's gone…"

Pg53   UC Spot & DSL
Both areas quite pale and tightly lit, UC cooler
Cue: Final "Say, do you believe in love?"

Pg53   Kill UC Spot
Cue: "From your affectionate mother, Joan Durbeyfield."

Pg54   DSR only
Quite pale
Cue: "I think I ought to make him even now."

Pg56   Wedding
Day, very heightened and strained, almost unpleasantly bright to reflect artificiality of occasion – everyone trying to be jolly and putting a brave face on to mask their true emotions
Cue: "I do not, Tessy, really."

Pg57   D'Urberville mansion
Evening, very stark and cold, no natural light, possible unpleasant-feeling firelight
Cue: "…go to ground as the heart comes alive."

Pg59   b/o   Slow fade with end of music, possibly go to unpleasant-feeling firelight, then fully black?
Cue: "Had my innocence betrayed…"

-      preset   as above

Act 2

-      b/o
Cue: clearance

Pg60   Entr'acte
As Overture

Pg60   D'Urberville mansion
As above
Cue: end of entr'acte

Pg62   D'Urberville mansion (transition)
As above but sense of hours passing to the next morning, some weak autumnal light
Cue: "...going to live with me long, are you, Angel?"

Pg63   Carry Me Home
Outdoors, weak autumnal light; "long shadows comb" – sense of loss, desolation, isolation, depression
Cue: "- don't make it more than I can bear!"

Pg65   Cottage exterior
As above but weak autumnal light (add in cottage exterior to Carry Me Home)
Cue: "Here – let me guide you, Carry me home"

Pg66   Cottage interior
As above but even dourer
Cue: Durbeyfield family exits DSL

Pg67   Parsonage interior
As above

Cue: "Give it to Mother, mind..."

Pg69   Mountainside Farm
Desperately bleak winter's day, totally exposed to the elements, bitterly cold
Cue: "I like to think it's so..."

Pg71   Church
Fairly warm and cosy, well-lit
Cue: "I will go to his family at Emminster this Sunday coming."

Pg72   Country Lane
Winter, stark and very cold
Cue: Alec runs out USR after Tess

Pg75   Mountainside Farm
As above but distorted and shadowy
Cue: "...power over me already for me not to fear them."

Pg75   Mountainside Farm 2
As above but without the shadowy distortion
Cue: "You'll find us tame"

Pg77   Cottage interior
As above but even dourer
Cue: "Father? O, Father!"

Pg78   Cottage exterior
As above but full stage
Cue: "I beg and scrape and bleed..."

Pg79   Kingsbere
Winter's evening, extremely cold and very dark
Cue: Durbeyfield family enter

Pg80   Vaults
Eerie, shadowy and ghostly, very oppressive, no natural light
Cue: "...place of our ancestors find us a roof."

Pg83   Parsonage interior
As above
Cue: "End their suffering here..."

Pg84   SR Spot
As above but with SR spot added
Cue: "Only the one..."

Pg85   Country Lane
Spring, moderately bright.................
Cue: "...by the name of Alec D'Urberville."

Pg86   Trantridge interior
As above
Cue: Lisa-Lu shows Angel in

Pg87   Sandbourne
Spring day by the sea
Cue: "Thank you!"

Pg88   Boarding-house
Cold and faded
Cue: Landlady enters

Pg89   US Spots – DS lit dimly
Silhouettes of Tess and Alex
Cue: "Go!"

Pg90   Kill US spots
Cue: Crashing sound

Pg91   UC Spot up full
Light Alec's broken body through gauze
Cue: Landlady screams

Pg92   Railway Station 2
Fairly bright Spring morning, smoke machine
Cue: a beat after Landlady exits

Pg93   Country Lane
As above but evening
Cue: "I feel strong enough to walk any distance!"

Pg94   Manor
Interior   rich, intimate, fairly dark but very warm and comforting,
area around Tess and Angel grows in intensity throughout song
Cue: "Come, let us see if we can't climb inside..."

Pg96   Stonehenge
Midnight, moonlit, pagan, otherworldly
Cue: "Once more"

Pg96   Dawn
Light grows very slowly on "altar" where Tess lies like a sacrifice to the gods
Cue: "And I wanted to see you again – so very much!"

Pg101   Gaol
The gallows
Cue: "You'll find us tame"

Pg101   B/O save spot on Tess
Cue: Final drum beat of "Stony Ground" sequence

Pg 102   Crossroads
Late May evening, warm and pleasant, with a surreal tinge
Cue: a moment after the end of "Stony Ground"

Pg103 Village Green
Later the same evening, warm, rich, earthy and welcoming – a pagan fertility ritual, with a surreal tinge....
Cue: "Good evening, Sir John"

Pg103   Spot highlighting Angel and Tess
Cue: Angel takes Tess in his arms

Pg104   b/o
Cue: Final "Children of the earth!"

THIS
IS
NOT
THE
END

Lightning Source UK Ltd.
Milton Keynes UK
UKHW02f1051140218
317856UK00006B/260/P

9 780573 180040